Thomas MacKellar

Hymns and Metrical Psalms

Thomas MacKellar

Hymns and Metrical Psalms

ISBN/EAN: 9783744783781

Printed in Europe, USA, Canada, Australia, Japan

Cover: Foto ©Lupo / pixelio.de

More available books at **www.hansebooks.com**

Faith, Hope, Love, these Three.

HYMNS

AND

METRICAL PSALMS

BY

THOMAS MACKELLAR,
PH. D.

✢ ✢ ✢

PHILADELPHIA:
PORTER & COATES.
1893.

High and mighty God and Saviour!
On the earth thy will be done:
Hallowed be thy name forever,
Holy Father, Holy Son,
Holy Spirit!
Lord Jehovah!
Glory be to Thee alone.

THIRD EDITION.

THE new Hymns in this edition are Nos. XXVIII., XL. and LXXXVII. to CII., and the additional Psalms are the 10th, 86th, 92d, 93d, and 100th. Some alterations have been made in the earlier-written pieces.

T. McK.

GERMANTOWN, PA.
January, 1893.

FIRST EDITION.

*S*OME of the Hymns in this volume were written before a busy life had passed its noontide; others, when the rays of the westering sun were falling slantwise.

Every piece that may be deemed worthy is freely at the service of the church.

April, 1883.

First Lines.

	PAGE
After the darkness of the night	40
Again I take with hopeful heart	52
A gladsome heart is mine this day	207
Alone with God to-day	34
A prisoner of the Lord	102
A refuge and a fortress	239
Art thou in thy spirit lowly	78
As children dwelling in their home	112
At Jesus' feet I take my place	124
At the door of mercy sighing	60
all unseen the master	*67*
Bear the burden of the present	88
Before the silver cord be loosed	178
Be not anxious for the morrow	30
Be not disquieted, my soul!	22
Be still, my soul! be still	188
Blessed be thy name forever	58
Book of grace and book of glory!	156
Bow down thine ear to me, O Lord!	244
Builder of thy holy church	194
Build up, O Lord, a rampart-wall	171
Cast thy burden on the Lord	132
Christ is risen! O the wonder!	139
Cold the bed and hard the pillow	183
Day is breaking in the sky	16
Day is waning into shadow	180
Day of wrath! the day that endeth	198

	PAGE
Do the blest in Paradise.	218
Draw nigh to the Holy	66
Drifting on a lawless ocean	209
Elijah stood upon the mount.	92
Evermore Jehovah reigneth!	250
Far away the Saviour saw me.	46
Father! all is of thy giving	185
Father! in my life's young morning	150
Give ear unto my words, O Lord!	229
Give me a foothold on the rock.	126
Give me to know thy will, O God.	44
Glory be to God on high!	138
Glory to God in the highest!	13
God has said it,—and his promise	82
Ho, all ye lands! right joyfully.	253
How prone my hasty feet to stray.	216
I did not ask the reason why	205
I give myself to God	120
I have no hiding-place.	38
I know not when the Lord will call	160
I lift my longing eyes	254
I long for God, the living God	58
In tearless anguish once I lay	74
In the hidden ways of life.	114
In the midnight and the storm.	116
In the vineyard of our Father	146
In vain the ways of Providence	54
I thank the Lord my Maker.	152
It is a good thing to give thanks to the Lord	247

	PAGE
I will extol thee every day	256
I would I were content to be	20
JEHOVAH reigns! Let earth rejoice	251
Jesus! when my soul is parting	62
LET all the people sing a psalm	96
Lord of night as of the day!	204
Lord, take and lead me as a child	50
MY righteous God! O hear my call	227
My song of songs shall be	220
My soul cries out to God	48
My soul is resting in God's peace	64
My soul! why sit forsaken	166
NEARER to thy heart of love	164
No tears for those whose feet have pass'd	202
No tongue of man has ever told	108
O FATHER, for thy love!	174
O gracious Father! send us showers	72
O land of day, eternal day	136
O Lord, our Lord! in all the earth	231
O the agonizing prayer	130
O the blessedness of leaning	24
O the darkness, O the sorrow	176
Only in silence wait on God	242
Over the earth a stillness comes	94
REST and peace for Jesus' sake!	128
SITTING in the twilight musing	190
Some day the word will come to me	104
Sometimes, in quiet revery	134
Strength of our fathers in the day	192

	PAGE
THE billows round me rise and roll	70
The blessing of the Sabbath-day	106
The bright, the Morning-Star!	196
The darkness of the night came down	80
The day is wearing fast away	76
The day of wrath, that certain day	142
The dusty paths of earth defile	118
The heavens declare the glory	236
The morning of the centuries	42
The morning stars were singing	148
The pathway to the mercy-seat	122
The sea before, the foe behind	162
There is a land immortal	84
There is light on my path	158
Though darkness turn the skies to night	26
'Tis but a looking unto Christ	168
'Tis the Master standing yonder	222
'Tis well that thou, my God, shouldst be	86
UNSEEN by them, a glorious host	90
Upon the pillow of thy love	18
WAS Jesus tempted like as we	36
Watchers call'd to work for Jesus	32
What though the way be storm-begirt	28
When he waketh, when he sleepeth	100
Where could I go but unto thee	110
While some may run an easy pace	56
Who bids the wind to blow?	154
Who is he, my soul! that standeth	213
Who shall reign if not the Christ?	212
Who the love of God can measure?	225
Why standest thou far off, O Lord?	233
With a cruse of alabaster	68

HYMNS.

I. .... 8, 5.

A multitude of the heavenly host praising God, and saying, Glory to God in the highest.—Luke ii. 13, 14.

I.

GLORY to God in the highest!
    The day of all days
    Awakens our praise,—
    The thrice-blessed morn
    When Jesus was born,—
The name that the church glorifieth:
    Glory to God!
    Glory to God!
Glory to God in the highest!

II.

Glory to God in the highest!
    Let heaven resound
    To its uttermost bound
    With anthems of praise
    Both now and always,

While seraph to seraph replieth,
    Glory to God!
    Glory to God!
Glory to God in the highest!

III.

Glory to God in the highest!
    Let earth, with its hills,
    Its valleys and rills,
    Re-echo his praise
    Both now and always,
While mountain to mountain-top crieth,
    Glory to God!
    Glory to God!
Glory to God in the highest!

IV.

Glory to God in the highest!
    His goodwill and peace
    To men will not cease:
    The church lifts her voice
    While angels rejoice,
And her song with the seraphim's vieth:
    Glory to God!
    Glory to God!
Glory to God in the highest!

V.

Glory to God in the highest!
    The bountiful Lord,—
    The Father, the Word,
    The Spirit,—whose praise
    Both now and always
On the wings of infinity flieth:
    Glory to God!
    Glory to God!
Glory to God in the highest!

1821

II. . . . . 7's.

I laid me down and slept; I awaked; for the Lord sustained me.
Ps. iii. 5.

I.

DAY is breaking in the sky;
    Restful night has pass'd away:
Now I lift my early cry,
    Lead thy servant, Lord, to-day.

II.

Jesus, Master! forth I go,
    Taking up my 'custom'd task:
Teach me what I need to know,—
    Give me what I ought to ask.

III.

I see not the way before,
    But I go at thy command,
Entering gladly duty's door,
    Led by thy directing hand.

IV.

Take away my sin and guilt,
    Make me whiter than the snow:
Be my will just what Thou wilt,
    Asking not, Why is it so?

V.

May my soul, impell'd by love,
    Do whate'er thy Spirit saith,
That my life this day may prove,
    Through thy grace, the power of faith.

VI.

Glory to Thee evermore!
    Glory in the uttermost!
Heaven and earth thy name adore,
    Father, Son, and Holy Ghost.

1881.

III. . . . . C. M.

Yea, thou shalt lie down, and thy sleep shall be sweet.—Prov. iii. 24.

I.

UPON the pillow of Thy love
    My weary head I lay,
Assured that watchers from above
    Will round about me stay.

II.

The weanéd child, subdued and still,
    Sleeps on its mother's breast;
So I, submissive to thy will,
    Lean on thy strength for rest.

III.

The sighs, and tears, and agony
    That marr'd the hours of day,
Subside as tempests on the sea
    In silence die away.

IV.

The restful peace of answer'd prayer
    Is in my chasten'd heart:
My fears, my sorrows, and my care
    At thy command depart.

V.

O Lord, my God, my strength, my hope,
    In thee I find repose:
Vouchsafe my grateful eyes shall ope
    As softly as they close.

1881.

IV. . . . . C. M.

The way of man is not in himself: it is not in man that walketh to direct his steps.—Jer. x. 23.

I.

I WOULD I were content to be
    Just as my Lord shall will,
So I with cheerful constancy
    His purpose may fulfil.

II.

O may I be content to lay
    My hourly griefs and cares
Upon His arm that every day
    His children's burden bears:

III.

Nor proudly strive to carry part
    And leave to Him the rest,
As if but half my weary heart
    Need lean on Jesus' breast.

IV.

Though I should ask the Lord to show
    Some greater things to do,
May I be ever quick to go
    On humble errands too:

V.

To run in haste, or waiting stand,
    Content to go or stay,
While watching for his guiding hand
    To point the fitting way.

VI.

Whatever work the day shall bring,
    May I set Thee before,
And give to Thee, O Christ, my King,
    The glory evermore.

1881.

V. . . . . C. M.

It shall come to pass, that at evening time it shall be light.
Zech. xiv. 7.

I.

BE not disquieted, my soul!
    The Lord of grace and power
In loving-kindness doth control
    Thy goings every hour.

II.

When sorrows fall, he wraps the heart
    The closer in his love:
If here he takes away a part,
    He'll give thee all above.

III.

Why tremble when thy God shall lay
    A shadow on thy path?
Not e'en the dark, distressful day
    Portends a night of wrath.

IV.

The heavy clouds that, dark and dun,
    Thine upward pathway hide,
Shall blaze with glory when the sun
    Goes down at eventide.

V.

The Morning-Star betimes will rise,
    And thou thy tent shalt fold,
And step with rapturous surprise
    Within the gates of gold.

1881.

VI. . . . . 8, 7, 4.

Cast thy burden upon the Lord, and he shall sustain thee.—Ps. lv. 22.

I.

O THE blessedness of leaning
   On a strength beyond thine own!
O the fulness of the meaning!
   O the sweetness of the tone!
     Cast thy burden
On thy loving Lord alone.

II.

Often weary, yet contending,—
   Beaten down, again to rise,—
On his help alone depending,
   Looking up with trustful eyes,—
     Cast thy burden
On the arm that built the skies.

III.

Take his easy yoke upon thee,
   Lowly be like him in heart:

Child, it was his love that won thee,
    Will he bid thee now depart
      With thy burden,
When thy soul is full of smart?

IV.

Long ago the word was written,
    Word to generations blest,—
Hear it, children sorely smitten,
    Hear it, ye of troubled breast,—
      Cast thy burden
On the Lord, who giveth rest.

<small>1881.</small>

VII. . . . . C. M.

When my spirit was overwhelmed within me, then thou knewest my path.—Ps. cxlii. 3.

I.

Though darkness turn the skies to night,
    Though sorrows fill the air,
Nor moon nor stars my pathway light,
    Yet thou art with me there.

II.

I cannot see thee, but I know
    A stronger arm than mine
Upholds me in the time of woe,—
    Jesus! that arm is thine.

III.

Though words may fail when I would pray,
    And mute I lift my hands,
Thou hearest what I cannot say,
    And Gabriel near me stands.

IV.

A just God and a Saviour, thou
    Art full of love and grace:
Before thy majesty I bow
    With glad and trustful face.

V.

Thy sovereign grace gives sweet relief,
    Dispelling faithless gloom,
And the dark chamber of my grief
    Becomes a sunny room.

1861.

VIII. . . . . C. M.

I will be with thee: I will not fail thee, nor forsake thee.
Josh. i. 5.

I.

WHAT though the way be storm-begirt,
    If Jesus lead thee on!
Thou shalt not suffer loss or hurt,
    Nor walk the path alone.

II.

Must thou do battle on the way?
    The arm of God is thine:
Does he unprop thine earthly stay?
    Upon that arm recline.

III.

Has he not pledged his word to save?
    Will he himself deny?
Will he not hold thee fast who gave
    His Son for thee to die?

IV.

The Father chasteneth whom he will,
    And some he wills to spare;
But not the less he loveth still
    The souls that meekly bear.

V.

O Lord, my timorous heart control;
    Forgive my doubt and sin:
Open the windows of my soul
    And let thy sunlight in.

1881.

IX. . . . . 8, 7.

Behold the birds of the heaven, that they sow not, neither do they reap, nor gather into barns; and your heavenly Father feedeth them. Be not therefore anxious for the morrow: for the morrow will be anxious for itself.—Matt. vi. 26, 34.

I.

Be not anxious for the morrow,
   Let the morrow have its cares:
Soul, be not forecasting sorrow;
   Grace is given to him who bears
Crosses that he does not borrow:
   God controls the unawares.

II.

Neither sowing, neither reaping,
   Gathering not to store away,
Birds are in the Father's keeping,—
   Cares he not when children pray?
Why then, faithless, sighing, weeping,
   Doubt him for the coming day?

III.

Lilies, toiling not nor spinning,
    Gleam in robes beyond compare:
Never king from time's beginning
    Had such glorious dress to wear:
Souls that cost his life in winning
    Christ will keep with loving care.

1881.

X. . . . . 8, 7, 4.

Blessed are those servants whom the Lord when he cometh shall find watching.—Luke xii. 37.
Watch ye, stand fast in the faith, quit you like men, be strong. 1 Cor. xvi. 13.

I.

WATCHERS call'd to work for Jesus,
 To the glory of his name,
In the field where'er he pleases
 Our glad services to claim,—
  Ever ready!
 This our watchword and our aim.

II.

Watching for the revelation
 Of his glory and his grace,
When the power of his salvation
 Shall subdue earth's rebel race,—
  Always watching,
 Always standing in our place.

III.

Watching for the coming morning,
    Resting in the Saviour's might,
Even now we see its dawning,
    See the shafts of heavenly light
        Pierce the darkness
That enwrapt the world in night.

IV.

Watching while our hands are doing;
    Loitering not on conquer'd ground;
Looking forward, still pursuing,
    While the golden trumpets sound;
        King eternal!
True to thee may we be found.

V.

Watching, hoping, toiling, praying,
    Till the victory is won,
May we then hear Jesus saying,
    "Toilers, rest! your work is done!"
        As we enter
Homes of rest beyond the sun.

1882.

XI. . . . . S. M.

Come, my people, enter thou into thy chambers, and shut thy doors about thee.—Isa. xxvi. 20.

I.

Alone with God to-day,
My soul subdued and still,
My thoughts ascend the upward way
To Moses' lonely hill.

II.

From Nebo's utmost height
Mine eyes look longingly
To the far distant land of light
Beyond the glassy sea.

III.

I seem no stranger there,
No traveller unknown:
For in that heavenly land so fair,
My Lord is on the throne.

IV.

Among the company
    Who serve Him day and night,
Dear ones who walk'd on earth with me
    Walk now in robes of white.

V.

Their work and waiting done,
    He call'd them of His grace;
Their higher service is begun
    Before the Saviour's face.

VI.

I cannot know while here
    The joys of that sweet place
Where bliss pervades the atmosphere
    As ether filleth space.

VII.

So I in gladness wait
    Before the Lord to-day,
While catching glimpses through the gate
    Of glory far away.

1881.

XII. . . . . C. M.

A high priest... that hath been in all points tempted like as we are, yet without sin.—Heb. vi. 15.

I.

WAS Jesus tempted like as we,
    The Holy One of God?
Were paths of pain and poverty
    By him, our Master, trod?

II.

In all his earth was there no place
    To lay his head upon,
A King of more than royal race,
    Yea, God's eternal Son?

III.

Did he, to save the world from sin,
    Go toiling all the day?
On Olivet, man's soul to win,
    Did he at midnight pray?

IV.

And did he in his sorest strait
  Receive the bitter cup,
When on the hill beyond the gate
  His life he offer'd up?

V.

While thus the sinless Saviour fared,
  Can I, dare I repine,
When sorrow, want, and death he shared
  To make salvation mine?

VI.

O child redeem'd by his own blood,
  Why yield to anxious care?
Thou canst not sink beneath the flood
  When Christ is walking there.

VII.

Think not thy Saviour does not see
  When Satan casts a dart:
No arrow ever wounded thee
  That did not pierce his heart.

VIII.

The great High Priest is touch'd by all
  Thy weaknesses and woes;
And he, when grievous sorrows fall,
  Sufficient grace bestows.

1881.

XIII. . . . . S. M.

O Lord, my strength, and my fortress, and my refuge in the day of affliction.—Jer. xvi. 19.

I.

I HAVE no hiding-place,
   No refuge from the blast,
But in the arms of Jesus' grace
   Around about me cast.

II.

Though I see not His hand,
   I feel its loving power:
And guardian angels near me stand
   In my distressful hour.

III.

I dare not look within,
   But heavenward turn my gaze;
And lest my grief become my sin,
   My tongue breaks out in praise.

IV.

Though tears mine eyes bedim,
He dries the tears I shed;
And in my soul I sing a hymn,
Content and comforted.

1880.

XIV. . . . . 8, 7, P.

Him that turneth the shadow of death into the morning.
Amos v. 8.

I.

AFTER the darkness of the night
    Light cometh in the morning;
After the winter and its blight
    Spring wakes in new adorning.

II.

After the sowing of the seed
    The harvest greets the reaper;
After the day of loving deed
    Soft rest enfolds the sleeper.

III.

After the tempest's course is run
    A calm pervades the waters;
After the work of life is done
    God calls his sons and daughters.

IV.

After the closing of the eye
    They wake with Christ in heaven;
After the final victory
    The crown of life is given.

1881.

XV. . . . . C. M.

So mightily grew the word of the Lord and prevailed.—Acts xix. 20.

I.

THE morning of the centuries
    Beheld a light arise,
That in their heavenly ministries
    Ne'er fell on angels' eyes.

II.

Through all the ancient days it seem'd
    A planet new-begun;
It grew in fulness till it beam'd
    A sun beyond the sun.

III.

When earth with clouds of sin was dark,
    It made an open way;
E'en where it glimmer'd as a spark,
    Some souls received the ray;

IV.

And they became the sons of God
    Amid a scoffing race;
While bloody was the way they trod,
    His peace lit up their face.

V.

They seal'd their constancy with blood;
    And where the martyrs died
A multitude arose and stood,
    And God was glorified.

VI.

That sun has never ceased to shine
    Upon the King's domain,
Pouring from heaven a light divine
    To make its pathway plain.

VII.

Till centuries shall be no more,
    Its light shall not grow dim;
And Christ's redeem'd on heaven's shore
    Shall sing redemption's hymn.

1881.

XVI. . . . . C. M.

Order my steps in thy word; and let not any iniquity have dominion over me.—Ps. cxix. 133.

I.

GIVE me to know thy will, O God,
    And may I see to-day
A light from heaven upon my road
    To clearly point the way:

II.

That I may know just what to do,
    And what to leave undone,
And be unto thy service true
    From dawn to setting sun:

III.

That I may speak the timely word,
    And timely silence keep,—
By passion's hasty words unstirr'd
    That cause the soul to weep:

IV.

That I may hold my thoughts in check,
    And every wild desire
That rises quick at pleasure's beck
    And flames into a fire:

V.

That I may kiss the needed rod,
    And patient bear the blow;
And say, 'Tis from the love of God;
    My Father wills it so.

VI.

Lord Jesus! from thy holy place
    The Spirit on me breathe:
Open the mantle of thy grace
    And keep my soul beneath.

1880.

XVII. . . . . 8, 7, 4.

But while he was yet afar off, his father saw him, and was moved with compassion.—Luke xv. 20.

I.

FAR away the Saviour saw me,
    Lost and wandering in the wild:
By his love he sought to draw me,—
    Me unworthy and defiled,—
        As a father
Calls to him his erring child.

II.

I saw not the hand that beckon'd,
    I heard not his gracious call,
Till the joys on which I reckon'd,
    Worldly joys, had perish'd all;
        Then his mercy
Led me at his feet to fall.

III.

Jesus broke the chains that bound me,
    And his freeman I became:
Robes of grace he threw around me,
    Covering all my sin and shame:
        O how precious
    Is my great Deliverer's name!

IV.

Over all and bless'd forever,
    God on his eternal throne,
Who the bond of love can sever
    That unites to Christ his own?
        Lord Jehovah!
    Glory be to Thee alone.

1882.

XVIII. . . . . S. M.

O my God, my soul is cast down within me.—Ps. xlii. 6.

I.

MY soul cries out to God,
    Like children in the night,
Who fear some evil is abroad
    Because they see no light.

II.

There's darkness on the path,
    And pitfalls line the way,
Till fear of coming trouble hath
    An overpowering sway.

III.

It may be faith is weak;
    Perchance the heart is faint,
And in unutter'd words would speak
    Its longing, hungering plaint.

IV.

The duties left undone,
The follies unforgiven,
Rise up like clouds before the sun
And vail the face of heaven.

V.

So, desolate and lone,
The soul lifts up its cry
To Christ upon his gracious throne
Of majesty on high.

VI.

Lord, calm this restless mind,
From murmuring set me free,
And strength and comfort let me find
In earnest work for Thee.

1882.

XIX. . . . . C. M.

Therefore for thy name's sake lead me, and guide me.
Ps. xxxi. 3.

I.

LORD, take and lead me as a child
    That knows not how to go,
Alike when day is calm and mild
    And night's wild tempests blow.

II.

If grief and pain be mine to bear
    And sorrows bow my head,
Let not my heart sink in despair
    As though my Lord were dead.

III.

When I am weary, on the breast
    Of Him who died for me,
O let my laden spirit rest,
    From care and worry free.

IV.

When joy shall fill my earth and skies
    With a serenest calm,
Then may my thoughts to Thee arise
    In one continual psalm.

V.

When some sad brother turns to me
    In sore and heavy grief,
May I be quick in sympathy
    And quicker in relief.

VI

When some poor soul is sick of sin
    And seeks the way to God,
O make me wise that soul to win
    To take the heavenward road.

VII.

Lord, in the dark and in the light
    Still keep me in thy way,
A child whose hand is claspéd tight
    In thine by night and day.

1875.

XX. . . . . C. M.

Even there shall thy hand lead me, and thy right hand shall hold me.
Ps. cxxxix. 10.

I.

Again I take with hopeful heart
    My life's allotted task:
To do it well the grace impart;
    This, Lord, I humbly ask.

II.

The day's perplexing mysteries
    I may not understand:
Be it enough my Father sees
    And holds them in his hand.

III.

My duty for the day is plain,—
    To go where God shall call,
Or, patient, hold the tangled skein
    While he unravels all.

IV.

I may not ask that no rough wind
    Upon my head shall blow,
Yet I may pray that I shall find
    Strength in the day of wo.

V.

It may be night, it may be day,
    A path I ne'er have gone,—
Whate'er shall be thy time or way,
    My Father! lead me on.

1852.

XXI. . . . . C. M.

Canst thou by searching find out God? canst thou find out the Almighty unto perfection.—Job xi. 7.

I.

IN vain the ways of Providence
With anxious gaze we scan:
To find out God by human sense
It is not given to man.

II.

Enough to know he cannot err
When worlds his plans fulfil;
That not a blade of grass can stir
But at its Maker's will.

III.

Enough to know that God is just,
Yet with a father's heart;
Enough with loving faith to trust
When earthly friends depart.

IV.

Enough to know he gave his Son
  The sin and grief to bear
When men like sheep astray had gone,
  And none to help was there.

V.

The Lord is just, the Lord is good:
  His ways we cannot trace:
Yet he who as our ransom stood
  Is Lord of life and grace.

1882.

XXII. . . . . C. M.

Take thy part in suffering hardship, as a good soldier of Christ Jesus.—2 Tim. ii. 3.

I.

While some may run an easy pace
   With self-reliant boast,
The Lord e'er gives to those his grace
   Who seek and need it most.

II.

Beneath a quiet smile may lie
   A sorrow of the soul
That needs a daily victory
   To hold it in control.

III.

And they who bear the battle's brunt,
   And temper'd weapons wield,
Shall stand up grandly in the front
   And hold the conquer'd field.

IV.

God's rank and file, in battle line
    And truth's divine array,
Shall set their camp at day's decline
    Along the King's highway

V.

To that good land, by sense unknown,—
    That land whose name is Heaven,—
Where Christ doth gather all his own,
    And crowns of life are given.

1881.

XXIII. . . . . 8, 7, 4.

*Our Lord Jesus Christ . . . the blessed and only Potentate, the King
of kings, and Lord of lords; who only hath immortality, dwelling in
light unapproachable, whom no man hath seen, nor can see:
to whom be honour and power eternal. Amen.*
1 Tim. vi. 14-16.

I.

BLESSED be thy name forever,
    Lord and Christ, eternal King!
While we live, our tongues shall never
    Fail thy glorious praise to sing,—
      While before Thee
Thankful offerings we bring.

II.

In the fulness of the ages
    Thou as man didst come to earth:
Welcomed by the wisest sages,
    Israel saw not thy worth,—
      Yet what glory
Heralded thy wondrous birth!

III.

Scorn'd by cruel men, they slew thee,
    Thou the Maker of them all!
Though so few were they that knew thee,
    Blest were they whom thou didst call,—
        Like their Master,
    By the hand of man to fall.

IV.

Throned in thy eternal glory,
    Myriads worship at thy feet:
May we bend with them before thee
    When our work shall be complete,—
        By thy Spirit
    Made for heavenly service meet.

1883.

XXIV. . . . . 8, 7.

Come unto me, all ye that labour and are heavy laden, and I will give you rest.—Matt. xi. 28.

I.

At the door of mercy sighing
    With the burden of my sin,
Day and night my soul is crying,
    "Open, Lord, and let me in."
Waiting mid the darkness dreary,
    Stretching out my hands to Thee,
In the refuge for the weary
    Is there not a place for me?

II.

I have sought to earn thy favour,
    Caring not for toil or cost;
Yet I find not him my Saviour,
    Him who came to seek the lost.
Blessed Master! in thy pity
    Teach me what I ought to do,
So that in the holy city
    I may gain an entrance too.

III.

Hark! what sounds mine ear receiveth,
    Sweet as songs of seraphim!
"He that in the Lord believeth
    Life eternal hath in Him.
At the outer door why staying?
    Nothing, soul! hast thou to pay:
Christ in love to thee is saying,
    Weary child, come in to-day."

IV.

I knew not of Jesus' kindness!
    I knew not of Jesus' grace!
O the blackness of the blindness
    That could not behold his face!
I saw not the door was open,
    Nor my Lord invite me in:
Grace is mine beyond my hoping,
    Mercy mightier than my sin.

1871.

XXV. .... 8, 7, 4.

Fear not; I am the first and the last.... I am the Alpha and the Omega, the beginning and the end. I will give unto him that is athirst of the fountain of the water of life freely.
Rev. i. 17. xxi. 6.

I.

JESUS! when my soul is parting
    From this body frail and weak,
And the deathly dew is starting
    Down this pale and wasted cheek,—
      Thine, my Saviour,
    Be the name I last shall speak.

II.

Jesus! when my memory wanders
    Far from loved ones at my side,
And in fitful dreaming ponders
    Who are they that near me glide,—
      Last, my Saviour,
    Let my thoughts on thee abide.

III.

When the morn in all its glory
    Charms no more mine ear nor eye,
And the shadows closing o'er me
    Warn me of the time to die,—
        Last, my Saviour,
    Let me see thee standing by.

IV.

When my feet shall pass the river,
    And upon the farther shore
I shall walk, redeem'd for ever,
    Ne'er to sin—to die no more,—
        First, Lord Jesus!
    Let me see thee, and adore.

1848.

XXVI. . . . . C. M.

The peace of God, which passeth all understanding.—Phil. iv. 7

I.

MY soul is resting in God's peace,
    Without a care or fear:
The tumults of my bosom cease,
    For Christ my Lord is here.

II.

The Spirit poureth from on high
    A sanctifying tide;
And, bathing in its stream of joy,
    My soul is satisfied.

III.

He driveth curious doubts away,
    He giveth childlike faith;
And so I take the yea or nay
    Just as my Saviour saith.

IV.

I have not other wish to be
    Than what my Lord ordains;
So what He knoweth best for me,
    That be my richest gains.

V.

A spirit meek and quieted
    Is better than a crown;
How rich the blessing on the head
    That Jesus sendeth down!

VI.

Here in his banquet-house I bide,
    His banner o'er me love,
And wait the coming eventide
    Of perfect peace above.

1870

XXVII. .... 6, 5.

Draw nigh to God, and he will draw nigh to you.—James iv. 8.

I.

DRAW nigh to the Holy,
    Bend low at His throne;
There, penitent, lowly,
    Thy sinfulness own:
There, there, if thou yearnest
    For pardon and rest,
There, fervent and earnest,
    Prefer thy request.

II.

Confess thy backsliding,
    Thy weakness and fears;
In Jesus confiding,
    There pour out thy tears.
Think not He will scorn thee,
    Though wretched thy case;
His hands will adorn thee
    With garments of grace.

III.

More precious than treasure,
    More vast than the sea,
His love has no measure
    Nor limit to thee.
His easy yoke wearing,
    His pleasure abide;
In all thy cross-bearing,
    He'll walk by thy side.

IV.

Fear not the wild clangour
    That Satan may raise,
So God's righteous anger
    But pass from thy ways.
Whom Christ has forgiven
    Goes safely along,
Till in the high heaven
    He sings the new song.

V.

Then kneel to the Holy,
    Bend low at His throne;
There, penitent lowly,
    Thy sinfulness own:
There, soul! if thou yearnest
    For pardon and rest,
There, fervent and earnest,
    Prefer thy request.

XXVIII. . . . . 8, 7.

She brought an alabaster cruse of ointment.—Luke vii. 37.

I.

WITH a cruse of alabaster,
　　Full of spikenard rich and sweet,
Stands she weeping near the Master,
　　While her tears bedew his feet.

II.

Her soft hair, a silken towel,
　　Wipes away the vagrant tears,—
Tears her eager heart's avowal
　　Of a love that hath no fears.

III.

"Knows he not she is a sinner?"
　　Inly speaks the Pharisee
Who had bidden Christ to dinner
　　When he dwelt in Bethany.

IV.

Lost on her the sneer that hisses
　　Serpent-like within its den:
She with spikenard, tears, and kisses,
　　Laves the weary feet again.

V.

She a sinner, he the Saviour!
    Meet it is that she should come:
Who hath greater need of favour
    Than a soul that has no home?

VI.

Known to Christ her whole condition,
    At its best and at its worst,—
She who bends in meek contrition,
    She who is of man accurst.

VII.

O the mercy of the Master!
    O the pity of our Lord!
E'en the cruse of alabaster
    Is with grace and pardon stored!

VIII.

As the glorious bow in heaven
    Cheers the earth when tempests cease
So his words: "Thou art forgiven!
    Faith hath saved thee: go in peace!"

                                          1892.

XXIX. . . . . C. M.

What time I am afraid, I will trust in thee.—Ps. lvi. 3.

I.

THE billows round me rise and roll,
  The storms of worldly care
Beat heavily upon my soul,
  And shroud me in despair:
Forsaken, comfortless, betray'd,
  With none to succour me,—
Father! what time I am afraid,
  Then will I trust in Thee!

II.

As feeble as the bruisèd reed,
  Infirm to will or do;
Oft working out the ungrateful deed
  'Twere better to eschew;
How were the sinking soul dismay'd
  But for this refuge-plea,—
Father, what time I am afraid,
  Then will I trust in Thee!

III.

When hope is faint, and faith is weak,
    And fears the bosom fill,
And I a strong assurance seek
    That thou art gracious still;
I rest upon thy promise-word,
    To thine own truth I flee:
Father, what time I am afraid,
    Then will I trust in Thee!

IV.

When saintly paleness marks my face,
    And dimness fills mine eye,
And, hoping only in thy grace,
    I bow my head to die;
If, entering in the vale of shade,
    Nor sun nor star I see,
Father, what time I am afraid,
    Then will I trust in Thee!

1853.

XXX. . . . . C. M.

He prayed again; and the heaven gave rain, and the earth brought forth her fruit.—James v. 18.

I.

O GRACIOUS Father! send us showers,
    The gentle showers of rain,
To cheer the corn, the grass, the flowers,
    On mountain-side and plain.

II.

Command the pregnant clouds to rise
    And vail the fiery sun,
While from the fountains of the skies
    The streams of blessing run.

III.

O gracious Father! send us showers;
    The cattle mutely stand
Amid the scorch'd and wither'd bowers;
    Have mercy on our land!

IV.

The spider's web is on the mead,
    The worm consumes the leaf;
And all thy works before Thee plead
    The silent plea of grief.

V.

O gracious Father! send us showers;
    Regard our earnest cries;
But meek submission still be ours
    While our petitions rise.

VI.

To Thee each living thing looks up;
    Thou mad'st—thou'lt not destroy:
The overflow of mercy's cup
    Shall wake creation's joy.

1852.

XXXI. . . . . L. M.

For so he giveth his beloved sleep.—Ps. cxxvii. 2.

I.

IN tearless anguish once I lay,
   And every tender string of life
Was rudely smitten by disease,
   And nature quiver'd in the strife.

II.

To God I look'd for help the while
   The lingering moments seem'd to creep,
These words of grace broke on my mind,
   "He giveth his belovèd sleep."

III.

A gentle peace, like evening winds
   In summer from the ocean's breast,
Moved o'er my sighing, sinking soul,
   And soothed my murmurings all to rest;

IV.

And through that weary night of pain,
    When it were manliness to weep,
My soul was comforted by this,
    "He giveth his belovèd sleep."

V.

When prison'd long, my soul would fain
    Leap through her fragile walls and flee,
But on the unmeasured life beyond
    She, halting, gazes tremblingly;

VI.

Then may I simply trust in Him
    Whose arms his feeblest follower keep,
And close mine eyes, and say, in death,
    "He giveth his belovèd sleep!"

1842.

XXXII. . . . . C. M.

Or ever the silver cord be loosed, or the golden bowl be broken.
Eccl. xii. 6.

I.

THE day is wearing fast away,
  The night is coming on,
To end the earthly pilgrimage
  Begun at being's dawn.

II.

The voice of earthly friends no more
  Within my soul can reach;
Another world hath round me grown,
  Earth hath another speech.

III.

Now fain am I to go when He
  Who sent me here shall call:
I wait his gentle breath to cause
  The ancient tree to fall.

IV.

I long to lay my burden down,
    And in earth's bosom rest
As calmly as an infant sleeps
    Upon its mother's breast.

V.

Welcome, approaching shades of even,
    By idling triflers shunn'd!
I see the immortal life of heaven,
    And Christ, my God, beyond!

1840.

XXXIII. . . . .8, 7, 4.

Peter was grieved because he said unto him the third time, Lovest thou me? And he said unto him, Lord, thou knowest all things; thou knowest that I love thee.—John xxi. 17.

I.

Art thou in thy spirit lowly,
  Like the Man of Nazareth?
Art thou seeking to be wholly
    Join'd to him, come life, come death?
      Lov'st thou Jesus
    More than thine own vital breath?

II.

Is thy bosom full of sorrow?
  Is a cloud upon thy way?
Why the worldling's burden borrow?
    Child of grace and promise, say!
      Lov'st thou Jesus?
    Joy should be thy guest to-day.

III.

Hath God made all men to praise thee?
  Or art thou to fame unknown?
Only seek that he should raise thee
  Up to an immortal throne.
    Lov'st thou Jesus?
  He'll provide for all his own.

IV.

Care not thou how low thy station,
  If thy God hath chosen thee
Heir of glory and salvation
  Now and evermore to be!
    Lov'st thou Jesus?
  Life is thine eternally.

1870.

XXXIV. . . . . C. M.

Then he arose, and rebuked the winds and the sea; and there was a great calm.—Matt. viii. 26.

I.

THE darkness of the night came down
    And on my soul it lay,
As if my righteous Maker's frown
    Were gathering round my way.

II.

As lonely as if I alone
    In all the earth were left,—
As helpless as an infant-one
    Of mother's care bereft,—

III.

How swift and sure had been my doom
    Had Christ forgotten me!
A voice arose amid the gloom,
    "Thy Saviour loveth thee!"

IV.

Immediately there was a calm,
    A calm without, within;
For Jesus wrote upon my palm
    Full pardon of my sin.

V.

The inward tempests rage no more,
    The spirit's sorrows cease,
When Jesus stands upon the shore,
    And gently whispers, "Peace!"

1846.

XXXV. . . . . 8, 7, 4.

I shall give thee the heathen for thine inheritance, and the uttermost parts of the earth for thy possession.—Ps. ii. 8.

I.

GOD has said it,—and his promise
　　Stands as firmly as his throne,—
Earth shall be a sure possession
　　Granted to his Son alone;
　　　　And the heathen
Jesus' gracious reign shall own.

II.

Where a soul in guilt is lying,
　　There his gospel shall be sent;
Life and grace for wretches dying,
　　Balm for bosoms sad and rent:
　　　　News of mercy,
All shall hear the call, Repent!

III.

Thou the Lord of all creation,
  Every living soul is thine:
May the grace of thy salvation
   On the lands of darkness shine:
      Holy Spirit!
   To thyself the world incline.

IV.

Words of precious promise, spoken
   In thy faithfulness and love,
Never, never can be broken
   While thou reignest King above:
      Let thy mercies
   Thy abounding goodness prove.

1841.

XXXVI. . . . . 7, 6.

Yea, though I walk through the valley of the shadow of death, I will fear no evil: for thou art with me; thy rod and thy staff they comfort me.—Ps. xxiii. 4.

I.

THERE is a land immortal,
    The beautiful of lands;
Beside its ancient portal
    A silent sentry stands:
He only can undo it,
    And open wide the door;
And mortals who pass through it
    Are mortal nevermore.

II.

That glorious land is Heaven,
    And Death the sentry grim:
The Lord thereof has given
    The opening keys to him;
And ransom'd spirits, sighing
    And sorrowful for sin,
Pass through the gate in dying,
    And freely enter in.

III.

Though dark and drear the passage
    That leads unto the gate,
Yet grace attends the message
    To souls that watch and wait;
And at the time appointed
    A messenger comes down,
And guides the Lord's anointed
    From cross to glory's crown.

IV.

Their sighs are lost in singing;
    They're blessed in their tears:
Their journey heavenward winging,
    They leave on earth their fears.
Death like an angel seeming,
    "We welcome thee!" they cry:
Their eyes with rapture gleaming,
    'Tis life for them to die.

1845.

XXXVII. . . . . L. M.

It is God which worketh in you both to will and to work, for his good pleasure.—Phil. ii. 13.

I.

'TIS well that thou, my God, shouldst be
    The master of my destiny;
For were my lot placed in my hand,
Where should my sure salvation stand?

II.

Beset around with wily snares,
And cumber'd with uncounted cares,
What arm but thine alone can hold
My soul within thy saving fold?

III.

The things of sense allure mine eyes,
And sudden sins my soul surprise:
Were I no more thy grace to share,
Then naught were left me but despair.

IV.

I know that I am safe with thee;
Then in thy hands my portion be:
I cannot fear what may betide
When on thyself my hopes abide.

V.

Let sinless ones on merit stand,
I seek for mercy at thy hand:
No other way of help I see,
Thy grace in Christ must work for me.

VI.

A wretch were I to lean upon
The works my erring hands have done:
I stand a suppliant, with the plea,
Atoning blood was shed for me.

VII.

O let thy Spirit day by day
Uphold me in the upward way:
Enough for me that thou wilt keep
The feeblest of thy chosen sheep.

1846.

XXXVIII. . . . . 8, 7.

Let not your heart be troubled: ye believe in God, believe also in me.
John xiv. 1.

I.

BEAR the burden of the present,
    Let the morrow bear its own;
If the morning sky be pleasant,
    Why the coming night bemoan?

II.

If the darken'd heavens lower,
    Wrap thy cloak around thy form;
Though the tempest rise in power,
    God is mightier than the storm.

III.

Steadfast faith and hope unshaken
    Animate the trusting breast;
Step by step the journey's taken
    Nearer to the land of rest.

IV.

All unseen, the Master walketh
    By the toiling servant's side:
Comfortable words he talketh,
    While his hands uphold and guide.

V.

Grief, nor pain, nor any sorrow
    Rends thy breast to him unknown;
He to-day and He to-morrow
    Grace sufficient gives his own.

VI.

Holy strivings nerve and strengthen,
    Long endurance wins the crown:
When the evening shadows lengthen,
    Thou shalt lay the burden down.

1852.

XXXIX. . . . . C. M.

A host compassed the city both with horses and chariots.
2 Kings vi. 15.

I.

UNSEEN by them, a glorious host
  About God's people stand:
The heavenly watchers hold the post
  At his supreme command.

II.

There is no child of God too high
  To need their constant care,
And none too deep in poverty
  Their daily help to share.

III.

When loved ones go, and earth is lone,
  As if no friend were near,
Then unseen angels from the throne
  Bring helpful words of cheer.

IV.

The sun of hope breaks through our gloom,
    And wondering whence it came,
We start, like Mary at the tomb
    When Jesus call'd her name.

V.

When morning dawns, the darkness flies:
    When showers at evening fall,
A rainbow links the earth and skies:
    Our God is over all.

1882.

XL. . . . . C. M. P.

And after the fire, a still small voice.—1 Kings xix. 12.

I.

ELIJAH stood upon the mount:
　　Behold, the Lord pass'd by:
A great strong wind the mountain rent,
　　The shiver'd rocks did fly:
Jehovah was not in the wind,—
　　Behold, the Lord pass'd by.

II.

After the wind an earthquake crash'd,
　　As if the end were nigh:
Not in the earthquake was the Lord
　　Before the prophet's eye:
Not in the earthquake nor the wind,—
　　Behold, the Lord pass'd by.

III.

After the earthquake, flaming fire
　　Encrimson'd earth and sky:

The wind that rent, the earthquake throe,
    The fire that flamed on high,
In none of them Jehovah was,—
    Behold, the Lord pass'd by.

IV.

When earthquake, wind and fire had ceased,
    And there was not a sound,
In tones of gentle stillness spake
    A still small voice profound:
Elijah, in his mantle wrapt,
    Stood there on holy ground.

V.

Not in the roar, the crash, the flame,
    Around, beneath, above,
The Lord in state majestic comes
    The heart of man to move:
His Holy Spirit conquers by
    The still small voice of love.

1892.

XLI......8, 7, P.

The Lord is good to all; and his tender mercies are over all his works.—Ps. cxlv. 9.

I.

OVER the earth a stillness comes,
    The eventide is falling:
Lord, bless all dwellers in their homes
    Who on thy name are calling.

II.

Thy blessing on the toiler rest;
    The over-worn and weary;
The dying, and the comfortless
    To whom the earth is dreary.

III.

Thy blessing on the child to-night;
    Thy blessing on the hoary;
The maiden clad in beauty bright,
    The young man in his glory.

IV.

Thy blessing on my fellow-race,
    Of every clime and nation:
May they partake thy saving grace,
    O Giver of salvation.

V.

If any man have wrought me wrong,
    Still blessings be upon him:
May I in love to him be strong,
    Till charity have won him.

VI.

Thy blessings on me, from of old,
    My God! I cannot number:
I wrap me in their ample fold,
    And sink in trustful slumber.

1853.

XLII. . . . . L. M.

Take a psalm, and bring hither the timbrel, the pleasant harp with the psaltery.—Ps. lxxxi. 2.

I.

LET all the people sing a psalm,
   A stately psalm of solemn praise,
While sitting in the holy calm,
   The calm befitting Sabbath days.

II.

Come, chant the words King David sang
   When heavenly airs around him swept,
And Zion's tents with music rang,
   While holy day the singers kept.

III.

The King of glory on his throne,
   The Ancient of eternal days,
The Lord Jehovah he alone,
   Immortal strains become his praise.

IV.

Let all the tribes of Adam's race,
    With thankful voice and lifted palms,
E'er magnify his truth and grace
    And laud him in the ancient psalms.

1868.

XLIII. .... C. M.

If any man thirst, let him come unto me, and drink.—John vii. 37.

I.

I LONG for God, the living God;
    I hunger for his grace:
I long to see as I have seen
    My heavenly Saviour's face.

II.

The earth has not a home for me
    Where I would always stay:
O let me take my pilgrim-staff
    And speed my upward way.

III.

I would not be afraid to live,
    Nor yet afraid to die;
Nor wish to end my working days,
    Or make them faster fly.

IV.

But I would hide myself beneath
    Jehovah's sheltering wing,
And wait till his appointed hour
    Shall life immortal bring.

V.

Lord, may I learn to work or wait,
    Just as thy word is given,—
Not loitering idly at the gate
    That opens into heaven.

1866.

XLIV..... 8, 7.

Whom the Lord loveth he chasteneth, and scourgeth every son whom he receiveth.—Heb. xii. 6.

I.

WHEN he waketh, when he sleepeth,
    When he toileth in the day,
Him the Father safely keepeth
    Who makes Christ his only stay.

II.

If he wanders, God will chasten
    Him with many stripes or few,
Till his erring footsteps hasten
    To the mercy-seat anew.

III.

If he meekly beareth crosses,
    And his eyes yet look to heaven,
God will turn to gain his losses,
    Yea, to him will much be given.

IV.

Daily he will find a token
    That his Lord loves to the end:
When the golden bowl is broken,
    Up to him shall he ascend.

V.

No more sin and no more sorrow,
    No more bitter tears to shed;
Heaven will have no sad to-morrow,
    But eternal day instead.

1882.

XLV.....S. M.

The Lord will strengthen him upon the bed of languishing.
Ps. xli. 3.

I.

A PRISONER of the Lord,
   Awaiting his commands,
My prison-house is amply stored
   With bounties from his hands.

II.

He makes my pillow soft
   While prostrate, weak, and sore,
And ministering angels oft
   Enter my chamber-door.

III.

Sweet love in every tone
   Is whisper'd round my bed:
I know that none will give a stone
   Instead of strengthening bread.

IV.

No fears my soul alarm;
  My pains shall pass away:
Christ puts his everlasting arm
  Beneath me all the day.

V.

How can I be cast down?
  Why wrap myself in gloom,
And wear a care-begotten frown,
  When Christ is in the room?

VI.

God's strokes are not in wrath:
  The fruits that feed the soul
Bestrew the strait and narrow path
  Unto the heavenly goal.

1882.

XLVI. . . . . L. M.

Secretly saying, The Master is here, and calleth thee.—John xi. 28.

I.

SOME day the word will come to me,
  Arise; the Master calls for thee.
May I be ready then to go,
Saying, Lord Jesus! even so.

II.

Will work I've purposed in my thought
Be to my Master's pleasure wrought?
And will more talents then be won,
So that the Lord may say, Well done?

III.

Will tears be shed upon my bier
By some I've help'd to comfort here?
Will seed I've sown some fruitage bear
Too late for me the joy to share?

IV.

Shall I on Jordan's farther side
Find some redeem'd and glorified
To whom I pointed out the road
Leading to that divine abode?

V.

I cannot answer Yea or Nay:
This only, Master, can I say:
If I've done aught to honour thee,
It was thy grace that wrought through me.

VI.

O blessed Lord, in me abide
When I pass over Jordan's tide,
That I with my last trembling breath
May glorify thy name in death.

1882.

XLVII. . . . . C. M.

On that day, the first day of the week, . . . Jesus came and stood in the midst.—John xx. 19.

I.

THE blessing of the Sabbath-day
   Again our spirit cheers,
And heaven seems not so far away
   That on our listening ears

II.

Some sounds of music may not fall
   Struck on angelic lyres,
Some anthems to the Lord, by all
   The high celestial choirs.

III.

Let our lips, too, break forth in praise
   To thee, O King of heaven,
For this the chiefest of the days,
   The holiest of the seven.

IV.

O Thou who on this day didst rise
    Omnipotent above,
Reveal to our expectant eyes
    New glimpses of thy love.

V.

Come, Holy Comforter, and show
    Thy gracious sovereign power,
That we may more like Jesus grow
    In this accepted hour.

VI.

As on the day of Pentecost,
    Visit thy church again,
That earth may join the heavenly host
    In praising Thee. Amen.

1882.

XLVIII. . . . . C. M.

Things which eye saw not, and ear heard not, and which entered not into the heart of man.—1 Cor. ii. 9.

I.

NO tongue of man has ever told
   God's everlasting love;
No heart has known the manifold
   Delights prepared above.

II.

Nor eye has seen, nor ear has heard,
   Nor mind has yet explored,
What things are token'd in his word
   For all that love the Lord.

III.

His children daily something learn
   While training in his schools:
Yet dimly do their minds discern
   How gracious are his rules:

IV.

Yet little can they apprehend
    What God has still in store;
For that which has no bound nor end
    They cannot reckon o'er.

V.

Glory to thee, eternal King!
    Invisible, yet known
To loving souls who daily bring
    Faith's offering to thy throne.

1882.

XLIX. . . . . C. M.

Jesus said therefore unto the twelve, Would ye also go away?
John vi. 67.

I.

WHERE could I go but unto thee,
    O man of Nazareth?
Thy blood was shed on Calvary
    To give me life for death!

II.

To whom, my Lord, but unto thee,
    O Son of God most high,
When angels bend with reverent knee
    Before thy majesty?

III.

Where can I go but unto thee,
    The only refuge-tower
Impregnable, where I can flee
    In sore temptation's hour?

IV.

To whom need I go but to thee?
    Thou art the utmost sum
Of every soul's necessity;—
    And therefore, Lord, I come.

V.

O Lamb of God, who cam'st to take
    The sin of man away,
Fast hold me for thy mercy's sake,
    And I shall never stray.

1882.

L. . . . . C. M.

For as often as ye eat this bread, and drink the cup, ye proclaim the Lord's death till he come.—1 Cor. xi. 26.

I.

As children dwelling in their home
    By right of grace divine,
Unto thy table, Lord, we come
    To take of bread and wine.

II.

The bread shows forth thy body slain,
    The wine thy blood out-pour'd:
To take away our sin and stain
    Cost thy dear life, O Lord.

III.

O may the Holy Ghost descend
    With blessing from above,
That grateful praise may now ascend
    For thine amazing love.

IV.

Abide with us this holy day
    And fill us with thy peace,
And while we gladly praise and pray,
    Lord, make our faith increase.

V.

Sit with us at the blessed feast,
    As in the day of old,
Our high and sovereign Saviour-Priest,
    Thy glory to behold.

1882.

LI. . . . . 7's.

There was at the table reclining in Jesus' bosom one of his disciples, whom Jesus loved.—John xiii. 23.

I.

IN the hidden ways of life
   God's belovéd may be found,
Shut in from the things of strife,
   Hedged with mercies all around.

II.

Born of God they know not when,
   Single is the faith they hold,
Prying not with curious ken
   Into what has not been told.

III.

Like the saint of Patmos isle,
   In them love has potent sway,
Israelites who have no guile,
   Passing on their heavenward way:

IV.

By the loving, kindly deed,
    By the strengthening word of cheer,
By the helpful hand in need,
    Glorifying Jesus here.

V.

Pointing out the path to heaven,
    Winning souls is their reward:
When the welcome-call is given,
    Dying, they wake in the Lord.

1882.

LII. .... 7's.

After ye were enlightened, ye endured a great conflict of sufferings.
Heb. x. 32.

I.

IN the midnight and the storm
    Some of God's beloved must go;
Not for them the valleys warm,
    But the hills of crag and snow.

II.

In the darkness call'd to stand,
    Fighting with a foe unseen,
Friend nor lover at their hand,
    Strongly on their Lord they lean.

III.

Chasten'd sore, bereaved, and lone,
    They with steadfast faith look up,
Seeking, low before his throne,
    Grace to take the bitter cup.

IV.

Not the less beloved are they,
    Heirs with Christ, who suffer loss:
They shall find, some coming day,
    Why 'twas theirs to bear the cross.

V.

Some the fight of faith must share:
    Some endure the tempter's blows;
Testimony they must bear
    Christ is mightier than his foes.

VI.

As they lay their weapons by,
    Conquerors in the final strife,
Glory be to God! they cry,
    Entering into restful life.

1882.

LIII. . . . . C. M.

Jesus answered him, If I wash thee not, thou hast no part with me.
John xiii. 8.

I.

THE dusty paths of earth defile
    My sandals through the day;
And vexing cares my soul beguile
    While toiling on the way.

II.

How oft I lose the gracious sense
    Of nearness unto Thee!
How oft forget the providence
    That orders life for me!

III.

The daily good that I would do
    Is often unbegun;
And evil I would fain eschew
    My heedless hands have done.

IV.

At eventime, unsatisfied,
    I call the day to mind;
And by thy righteous standard tried,
    Shortcomings do I find.

V.

O Thou who, in thy graciousness,
    Didst wash thy servants' feet,
Thy travel-stain'd disciple bless
    Before thy mercy-seat.

VI.

The robe of works that I have worn
    Is scanty for my needs:
Give me the robe of thy new-born,—
    Of faith and holy deeds.

1882.

LIV..... S. M.

Ye are not your own; for ye were bought with a price.
1 Cor. vi. 19, 20.

I.

I GIVE myself to God,
   My life, my soul, my all:
He knows the devious paths I've trod,
   In mercy's hand I fall.

II.

My sins I cannot count,
   Nor sum his favours up:
I humbly kneel at mercy's fount
   And take salvation's cup.

III.

I proffer but his own;
   And may the Master take
The gift I lay before his throne,
   For my Redeemer's sake.

IV.

I give myself to God,
   For evermore to hold:
I pass beneath the Shepherd's rod
   To bide within his fold.

1882.

LV.....C. M.

And him that cometh to me I will in no wise cast out.—John vi. 37.

I.

THE pathway to the mercy-seat
   Is found of all who will;
And they who kneel at Jesus' feet
   Find him a Saviour still.

II.

As, when upon the earth he trod,
   None empty went away
Who sought his blessing as their God,
   So we to him may pray.

III.

The child unto his parent runs
   For comfort and relief:
So may the Lord's redeeméd ones
   Go to him with their grief.

IV.

Yea, even in the busiest hour
    Unspoken prayer may rise,
And blessings in a gracious shower
    Fall on us from the skies.

V.

How wondrous 'tis that we may reach
    The heavenly throne by prayer!
That silent thought or utter'd speech
    Find gracious audience there!

1882.

LVI. . . . . C. M.

As many as touched him were made whole.—Mark vi. 56.

I.

At Jesus' feet I take my place:
    I touch his garment's hem:
A helpless child in need of grace
    My Lord will not condemn.

II.

I have no hope but in his love;
    His promise is my plea:
I give myself to Him who strove
    E'en unto death for me.

III.

I only ask that I may know
    What he would have me do,
That my obedient life may show
    The grace that bears me through.

IV.

I've nothing, Lord, to offer thee
    But what thou madest mine:
O take my all, and let it be
    Thine own, for ever thine.

1882.

LVII. . . . . C. M.

And the rock was Christ.—1 Cor. x. 4.

I.

GIVE me a foothold on the rock:
    The billows round me roll:
Let not their wild, impetuous shock
    O'erwhelm my trembling soul.
O Thou that walkest on the wave,
    Thou Ruler of the sea,
Stretch forth thy mighty arm to save
    The soul that calls on thee.

II.

Give me a foothold on the rock,
    O Saviour of the lost!
The world and sin my struggles mock,
    And I am tempest-tost.
I strive to reach an anchoring place:
    My God, give me a stay;
Extend to me thy hand of grace,
    Lest I be cast away.

III.

Give me a foothold on the rock,
　　Till voices 'yond the sea,
Like evening chimings of the clock,
　　Bid welcome home to me.
The day of toil and watching o'er,
　　The night of sorrow past,
I step upon the eternal shore,
　　And rest in peace at last.

1882.

LVIII. . . . . 7's.

The Lord lift up his countenance upon thee, and give thee peace.
Num. vi. 26.

I.

REST and peace for Jesus' sake!
    O my Father, hear my cry;
Heal my bosom's bitter ache,
    While before thy feet I lie.

II.

I have loved and I have lost
    Those whom I had prized too well:
O'er my threshold sorrow cross'd
    When the cherish'd idols fell.

III.

I forgot that they were lent,
    And I claim'd them as my own,
Till the message from thee sent
    Took them up before thy throne.

IV.

Speak the word of peace to me;
    Pardon thy forgetful child:
Let me find my rest in thee,
    Comforted and reconciled:

V.

Comforted, that loving eyes
    Shone so long within my home:
Reconciled, that to the skies
    Thou didst bid the loved ones come.

VI.

Rest and peace for Jesus' sake!
    Father, at thy feet I kneel:
Bruiséd reeds thou wilt not break,
    Thou the broken heart wilt heal.

1882.

LIX. . . . 7's.

Then cometh Jesus with them unto a place called Gethsemane.
Matt. xxvi. 36.

I.

O THE agonizing prayer
 Rising on the midnight air!
"Let this cup pass from thy Son:
Not my will, but thine be done!"
 Jesus in Gethsemane!

II.

O the tears and bloody sweat
Falling fast on Olivet!
In thy lonely agony,
Shedding crimson tears for me,
 Jesus in Gethsemane!

III.

O what wrath of earth and hell
On thy head unpitying fell,
When thy passion-time began,
Bearer of the sin of man,
 Jesus in Gethsemane!

IV.

Sorrow none had ever known
Came upon thy soul alone:
While its billows o'er thee swept,
Near at hand thy followers slept,
    Jesus in Gethsemane!

V.

Waken me from sinful sleep:
Faithful, loving, make me keep,
Watching every hour with thee
Who didst agonize for me,
    Jesus in Gethsemane!

VI.

Crimson'd once, but beauteous now,
O what glory crowns thy brow!
All the world shall bend the knee,
Lord triumphant! unto thee,
    Conqueror in Gethsemane!

1883.

LX. . . . . 7's.

Casting all your anxiety upon him, because he careth for you.
1 Peter v. 7.

I.

CAST thy burden on the Lord!
    Is this message meant for me?
May I take him at his word,
    And will he my helper be?

II.

In my daily household care,
    In the business of the day,
Will the Lord the burden bear
    Or his strength upon me lay?

III.

When the evil one shall cast
    Tempting baits to snare my soul,
Or shall taunt me with the past,
    Will the Lord his power control?

IV.

When the bitterness of grief
    Shall upon my bosom prey,
Will he give me swift relief?
    Will he take the pain away?

V.

When the parting hour is near,
    Will his everlasting love
Conquer every doubt and fear
    And the sting of death remove?

VI.

'Tis the promise of the Lord,
    Meant for me on every day:
Heaven and earth may fail,—his word
    Never once shall pass away.

1882.

LXI. .... C. M.

Behold, my servants shall sing for joy of heart.—Isa. lxv. 1.

I.

SOMETIMES, in quiet revery,
    When day is growing dim,
The heart is singing silently
    A sweet unwritten hymn.

II.

The strains are not to measure wrought
    By cunning of the mind,
But seem like hymnings angels brought
    From heaven, and left behind.

III.

The misty hills of bygone grief,
    Once dark to look upon,
Stand out like blessings in relief
    Against the setting sun.

IV.

The rain may fall, the wind may blow,
    The soul unhinder'd sings,
While, like the bird 'neath sheltering bough,
    She sits with folded wings,—

V.

A brief and pleasant resting space,
    A glance at Beulah land,
Before she girds herself apace
    For work that waits the hand.

VI.

Then, giving thanks to Him who pour'd
    Refreshment in her cup,
She hears the calling of her Lord
    And takes her labour up.

1882.

LXII..... C. M. P.

And there shall be night no more; and they need no light of lamp, neither light of sun.—Rev. xxii. 5.

I.

O LAND of day, eternal day,
    Unbroken by a night:
No need of candle nor of sun
Thy blessed fields to shine upon,—
    The Lamb of God thy light.

II.

O land of life that cannot die,
    To mortals open'd up:
No more the drooping of the eye,
The parting word, the fitful sigh,
    The bitter-tasting cup.

III.

O land of rest and sweet content,
    The time of battle o'er,

The weary victors, laying down
The cross, receive from Christ the crown
    To wear forevermore.

IV.

O land of beauty, beautiful
    Beyond the brightest dream
Of poet in his time of power:
No painter in his happiest hour
    Has caught its faintest gleam.

V.

Lord of the land! Eternal King
    Of a domain so fair!
O give us grace to watch and wait,
On duty at the outer gate,
    Till we may enter there.

1877.

LXIII. . . . . 7, 6, P.

Amen: Blessing, and glory, and wisdom, and thanksgiving, and honour, and power, and might, be unto our God for ever and ever.—Rev. vii. 12.

I.

GLORY be to God on high!
　　Glory in the highest!
Lord of wondrous majesty,
Maker of the earth and sky:
Saints redeem'd and angels cry,
　　Glory be to God on high!
　　Glory in the highest!

II.

　　Glory be to God on high!
　　Glory in the highest!
Father, Son, and Holy Ghost!
Praises in the uttermost
Earth shall sing with heaven's host:
　　Glory be to God on high!
　　Glory in the highest!

1883.

LXIV. . . . . 8, 8, 8.

Why seek ye him that liveth among the dead? He is not here, but is risen.—Luke xxiv. 5, 6.

I.

CHRIST is risen! O the wonder!
  Rending bands of death asunder,
Rising to the glory yonder!

II.

Silently as morning breaking
Came the wonderful awaking,
Christ again his Godhead taking:

III.

In the stillness of the morning,
Angels heralding no warning,
Though the world's new light was dawning.

IV.

Ere sunrising, one came seeking,
She whose heart with pain was reeking,
Tears her pallid cheek bestreaking.

V.

Last she saw him faint and dying;
Stark and cold her Lord was lying,
Ere she left him, weeping, sighing.

VI.

Lone she stood in tearful wonder:
Who had rent His tomb asunder?
Who so vile the grave to plunder?

VII.

She, amazed, her watch was keeping,
Blinding mists her vision steeping:
"Woman, why art thou a-weeping?"

VIII.

Was the startled woman chary?
Was she in her answering wary?
What a change when He said, "Mary!"

IX.

Once the piteous supplication,
Now the glad ejaculation,
"Master!" in rapt adoration.

X.

No more mocking, no more scourging,
Priest and mob the soldiers urging,
While the rage of hell was surging:

XI.

Crown of thorns no longer wearing,
Cruel taunts no longer bearing,
Nails no more his body tearing:

XII.

Majesty and gracious sweetness
Join in him with perfect meetness,
God and man in full completeness.

XIII.

Lord Jehovah! low before thee,
Ransom'd by thee, we adore thee:
Glory in the highest! Glory!

1882.

LXV. .... DIES IRÆ.

An attempt (based mainly on a literal rendering by J. Addison Campbell) to give in English verse the famous Latin hymn of Thomas of Celano, written in the thirteenth century.

I.

THE day of wrath, that certain day,
  In glowing embers earth shall lay,
Both David and the Sibyl say.

II.

With trembling dread the world will quake
Or e'er the Judge shall inquest make,
And ruin all things overtake.

III.

The trump shall sound a startling tone
Throughout the graves of every zone,
And call all men before the throne.

IV.

And death and nature in surprise
Shall see the creature man arise
To answer at the dread assize.

V.

The written book will forth be brought,
With good and evil records fraught,
And man be judged for deed and thought.

VI.

When he shall sit upon his throne,
The Judge will make all secrets known;
Things unavenged there shall be none.

VII.

And what shall wretched I then plead?
Who then for me will intercede,
When e'en the just will mercy need?

VIII.

King of tremendous majesty,
Who sav'st thine own by grace most free,
Thou fount of pity, rescue me!

IX.

Remember, Jesus kind, I pray,
Thou trod'st for me thy painful way:
Then do not lose me on that day!

X.

While seeking me, I wearied thee;
Thou on the cross redeemedst me:
In vain let not such travail be!

XI.

Just and avenging Judge, I cry,
Give me remission ere I die,
Before the reckoning-day comes nigh.

XII.

A culprit groaning with his care,
Guilt's crimson blush my face doth wear;
O God, the pleading suppliant spare!

XIII.

The sinful woman was forgiven,
And e'en the thief by thee was shriven;
Then give me also hope of heaven.

XIV.

My prayers, unworthy, do not spurn;
Thou who art good, in kindness turn,
Lest I in fire eternal burn.

XV.

Far from the goats' accursèd band
Keep me apart, and make me stand
Among the sheep at thy right hand.

XVI.

When, self-confuted, to their place
Of flame the wicked rush apace,
Then call my name with words of grace.

XVII.

Prostrate and suppliant, I cry,
While bruised in dust my heart doth lie,
O care for me that day I die!

Upon that day of tearful eyes,
When from the embers he shall rise,
And culprit man wait thy decree,
O God, then pardon even me.

    Kind Lord Jesus, ever blest!
    Give to thy redeeméd rest.
                Amen.

1882.

LXVI. .... 8, 7, 4.

A man had two sons; and he came to the first, and said, Son, go work to-day in the vineyard.—Matt. xxi. 28.

I.

IN the vineyard of our Father
 Daily work we find to do;
Scatter'd fruit our hands may gather,
 Though we are but weak and few:
  Little clusters
 Help to fill the basket too.

II.

Toiling early in the morning,
 Catching moments through the day,
Nothing small or lowly scorning,—
 So we work, and watch, and pray;
  Gathering gladly
 Free-will offerings by the way.

III.

Not for selfish praise or glory,
    Not for objects nothing worth,
But to send the blessed story
    Of the gospel o'er the earth,
        Telling mortals
    Of our Lord and Saviour's birth.

IV.

Up and ever at our calling,
    Till in death our lips are dumb,
Or till—sin's dominion falling—
    Christ shall in his kingdom come,
        And his children
    Reach their everlasting home.

V.

Steadfast, then, in our endeavour,
    Heavenly Father, may we be;
And forever, and forever,
    We will give the praise to thee;
        Alleluiah!
    Singing, all eternity.

                    1845.

LXVII. .... 7, 6.

The morning stars sang together, and all the sons of God shouted for joy.—Job xxxviii. 7.

I.

THE morning stars were singing
    With joy when time began;
And heavenly peals were ringing
    When God created man:
The universe was swelling
    With jubilant delight,
While all to all were telling
    The Lord Jehovah's might.

II.

A higher song of glory
    Was sung in after-days,—
And shepherds heard the story,
    As angels hymn'd His praise,—
Of Jesus in a manger,
    God's well-belovéd Son,
Who came to save from danger
    A race by sin undone.

III.

A multitude of voices
    Have learn'd this holy song;
And earth with heaven rejoices
    To roll the sound along.
With saints and angels o'er us,
    Singing before the throne,
We join the gladsome chorus,
    Glory to God alone!

1846.

LXVIII. . . . . 8, 7, 4.

Wilt thou not from this time cry unto me, My Father, thou art the guide of my youth?—Jer. iii. 4.

I.

FATHER! in my life's young morning,
    May thy word direct my way:
Let me heed each gracious warning,
    Lest my feet should go astray:
       Make me willing
All its precepts to obey.

II.

Father! gentle is thy teaching;
    Be a docile spirit mine:
Every day thy grace beseeching,
    Let thy loving-kindness shine
       Always on me,
And my heart be wholly thine.

III.

Father! let me never covet
   Things of vanity and pride:
Teach me truth, and may I love it
   Better than all else beside:
     Blessed Bible!
   May it be my heavenward guide.

1841.

LXIX. . . . . 7, 6.

Giving thanks always for all things.—Eph. v. 20.

I.

I THANK the Lord my Maker
   For all his gifts to me:
For making me partaker
   Of bounties rich and free:
For father and for mother,
   Who give me clothes and food,
For sister and for brother,
   And all the kind and good.

II.

I thank the Lord my Saviour
   Who came for me to die,
And bless me with his favour
   And fit me for the sky,—
That, all my sins out-blotted,
   By Jesus wash'd away,
I may be found unspotted
   When comes the final day.

III.

I thank the Lord for giving
    The Spirit of his grace,
That I may serve him living,
    And, dying, reach the place
Where Jesus in his glory
    I shall forever see,
And tell the wondrous story
    Of all his love for me.

1844.

LXX. . . . . H. M.

Thou makest the outgoings of the morning and evening to rejoice. Thou visitest the earth, and waterest it: thou greatly enrichest it with the river of God.—Ps. lxv. 8, 9.

I.

WHO bids the wind to blow?
    Who makes the sun to shine,
And flowers and grass to grow
    Around this path of mine?
Who makes these shady trees arise,
And spread their boughs beneath the skies?

II.

Who makes this brook, so bright,
    From earth's cold bosom spring,
And sparkle in the light,
    And sweetly, sweetly sing,
As if an angel lent his voice
To help the rippling stream rejoice?

III.

Who gave the airy bird
    Soft feathers and swift wings,
And taught it music-words
    To charm us when it sings?—
Say, little bird! who taught you how
To sing so sweetly on that bough?

IV.

O, 'tis our Father, God,
    Who gives us every thing:
The grass, the flowery sod,
    The brook, and birds that sing;
And all the blessings of this day
He sheds upon our happy way.

V.

How good is God! He gave
    His only Son to die,
Our souls from death to save,
    And fit us for the sky.
O, let us bow, and serve him here
With gratitude and love sincere.

1842.

LXXI. . . . . 8, 7, 8, 4.

Thy word is a lamp unto my feet, and a light unto my path.
Ps. cxix. 105.

I.

BOOK of grace, and book of glory!
    Gift of God to age and youth;
Wondrous is thy sacred story,
    Bright, bright with truth.

II.

Book of love! in accents tender,
    Speaking unto such as we;
May it lead us, Lord, to render
    All, all to thee.

III.

Book of hope! the spirit sighing
    Consolation finds in thee,
As it hears the Saviour crying,
    "Come, come to me."

IV.

Book of peace! when nights of sorrow
    Fall upon us drearily,
Thou wilt bring a shining morrow,
    Full, full of thee.

V.

Book of life! when we, reposing,
    Bid farewell to friends we love,
Give us for the life then closing,
    Life, life above.

1843.

LXXII. .... 6, 9.

"At the Beautiful Gate of the Temple."—Acts iii. 10.

I.

THERE is light on my path,
    There is joy in my heart,
For the doubt and the fear
    From my bosom depart,
While I muse on his love
    As I quietly wait
For the Master to come
    At the Beautiful Gate,
The Beautiful Gate of the temple.

II.

There is travailing care;
    There is labour in vain;
There is noise in the air;
    There is pitiless rain;

And I cover my head
    Till the storm shall abate,
And the Lord shall appear
    At the Beautiful Gate,
The Beautiful Gate of the temple.

III.

I am sorely beset;
    I am weary and worn;
And I sigh for the night,
    And I long for the morn:
He will come in good time,
    Whether early or late,
As I kneel for his touch
    At the Beautiful Gate,
The Beautiful Gate of the temple.

IV.

Lo! the darkness is past,
    And the morning is here;
'Tis the voice of my Lord
    That enraptures my ear:
He has come to my help
    In my uttermost strait,
And he beckons me in
    At the Beautiful Gate,
The Beautiful Gate of his temple.

1885.

LXXIII. . . . . 8, 9.

"Ye know not when."—Mark xiii. 35.

I.

I KNOW not when the Lord will call,
    Or in the night or in the morning:
The angel's foot may softly fall,
    Or it may give a note of warning.

II.

There may be but a step between
    Earth's outer gate and heaven's portal:
Or morn may slowly lift the screen
    That hangs before the day immortal.

III.

The Lord may whisper, "Follow me!"
    When none but I shall hear the calling,
And men may marvel when they see
    A tree in summer greenness falling.

IV.

Perchance I may be left to wait,
   His earlier-chosen taken only,
And I may feel 'tis getting late,
   And earth is growing dim and lonely.

V.

Perchance when gladsome days are come,
   Or when the wintry winds are blowing,
The Lord will bid me hasten home,
   Unquestioning and all unknowing.

VI.

The time, the way, I'd leave to Thee:
   Were mine the choice, this would I rather,
Content that both alike shall be
   As seemeth best to thee, my Father.

1885.

LXXIV. . . . . L.M.

"Whom God hath hedged in."—Job iii. 23.

I.

THE sea before, the foe behind,
  What place of hiding can I find?
Shut up from help on every side,
What hand my trembling feet will guide?

II.

From Satan's realm I sought to flee,
And now behold the raging sea!
The foe is pressing on me sore,
And I shall perish on the shore.

III.

When I set out to 'scape his sway
The guide-posts pointed me this way:
Is there no arm this side the wave
The hunted fugitive to save?

IV.

The treacherous deep my soul may snare,
And yet away far over there
The haven of salvation lies,
Its borders reaching to the skies.

V.

And must I venture in the sea?
Is there no other path for me?
Will the same hand that led me here
For my deliverance now appear?

VI.

O Lord, my Saviour! hear my cry:
In my distressful day come nigh:
Now, trembling, on the waves I tread,
O hold me in this time of dread.

VII.

The waters part before my feet;
Onward I press with footsteps fleet:
Dry-shod I reach the farther strand
And enter in Immanuel's land!

VIII.

Forevermore Thy praise I'll sing:
Glory to thee, Eternal King!
'Tis thine to order all my way,
Be mine unquestioning to obey.

1885.

LXXV. . . . . 7's.

"**Draw nigh unto my soul.**"—Ps. lxix. 18.

I.

NEARER to thy heart of love;
　Nearer to thy hand of power:
　Jesus! nearer every hour
Lift me to the life above.

II.

Nearer unto thee, my Lord,
　Who art always near to me,
　Though thy hand I may not see
As it guides me heavenward.

III.

Nearer to thy gracious throne
　May thy Spirit draw my feet,
　Nearer to thy mercy-seat,
Seeing none but thee alone.

IV.

Nearer when the morn shall break,
    Nearer when the sun goes down,
    Let thy loving-kindness crown
All the way my feet should take.

V.

Nearer in the crowded day,
    Nearer in the secret place,
    Let the sense of present grace
In my peaceful bosom stay.

VI.

Nearer when my trembling hand
    Lifts the dreaded cross with fear,
    Though I shed the human tear
When, bereft, I mutely stand.

VII.

Nearer, Jesus, to thy breast
    As my daily need is more,
    Till thou openest the door
Leading to the heavenly rest.

1885.

LXXVI. .... 7, 6.

"O my soul, why art thou disquieted within me?"—Ps. xlii. 11.

I.

MY soul! why sit forsaken
    In sorrow's darken'd tent?
Why should thy trust be shaken
    By griefs thy Lord hath sent?

II.

It was the love he bore thee
    That led him to the cross:
That love is ever o'er thee,
    To save thee, soul, from loss.

III.

Go, climb faith's sacred mountain,
    Unweighted by thy fears;
Arise above the fountain
    That feeds the stream of tears;

IV.

And thou shalt see far over
    The mist that dims thine eyes,
And then shalt thou discover
    The bow across the skies.

V.

It is not always raining;
    It is not always night:
His grace shall shame thy plaining;
    Thy God is always right.

VI.

In lovingness he reigneth
    O'er all his family,
And whatso he ordaineth
    Is ever best to be.

VII.

Then let thy night of sadness
    Bring in the grateful day,
And thou shalt walk in gladness
    With Jesus by the way.

1885.

LXXVII. .... C. M.

"Look unto me, and be ye saved."—Isaiah xlv. 22.

I.

'TIS but a looking unto Christ
    In penitence and trust,
And he bestows the grace unpriced
    That counts the sinner just.

II.

'Tis but a doing of his will,
    The work of faith in love,
And he the passing days shall fill
    With blessings dream'd not of.

III.

'Tis but the leaving in his hands
    The morrow with its cares,
And peace within the bosom stands
    An angel unawares.

IV.

'Tis but a word of comfort said,
    A simple, kindly deed,—
Yet 'tis a precious ointment shed
    Upon a soul in need.

V.

'Tis but the bearing patiently
    The wrongful word, the sneer,
And love shall turn the enmity
    Of hate's empoison'd spear.

VI.

'Tis but a look of tenderness
    On weepers left behind
That lingers evermore to bless
    The sad and lonely mind.

VII.

'Tis but the closing of the eye,
    The ceasing of the breath,
Then comes the hour of victory,
    The triumph over death.

VIII.

'Tis but a lifting of the latch
    That fastens glory's door,

And wondrous sights the eye shall catch
  On heaven's resplendent floor.

IX.

'Twas but an erring child of earth
  With mortal sandals shod:
Lo! now, of an immortal birth,
  He lives with Christ in God.

1885.

LXXVIII. . . . 8, 4.

"Hold thou me up, and I shall be safe."—Ps. cxix. 117.

I.

BUILD up, O Lord, a rampart-wall
    Along my way,
That, journeying onward, I withal
    Go not astray.

II.

Whene'er the road be rough and steep,
    And I, foot-sore,
Over the rocks but slowly creep,
    Give strength the more.

III.

When noon shall pour upon my brow
    Its burning heat,
Beside the shadowing rock guide Thou
    My faltering feet.

IV.

While walking lonely in the dark,
    No hand in mine,
Vouchsafe a star, a heavenly spark,
    On me to shine.

V.

When lost amid a tangled wild
    Of fear and doubt,
Good Shepherd, seek the erring child
    And lead him out.

VI.

The fruit of earth's forbidden trees
    Let me not taste;
Nor lag, nor lie in bowers of ease,
    When I should haste.

VII.

If e'er I meet one overborne
    Or faint of heart,
May I, instead of careless scorn,
    Good cheer impart.

VIII.

Let me not loiter on the edge
    Of any sin,
Lest, dallying on the slippery ledge,
    My feet slide in.

IX.

Yet, if unheedingly they slide,
    Thy grace I crave:
Be thou my rescuer and guide;
    Lord Jesus, save!

X.

When I come near, all worn and scarr'd,
    Thy mansions blest,
Then, Saviour, let me find unbarr'd
    The gate of rest.

XI.

Among the multitudes that throng
    The holy place,
Be mine to sing in loving song
    Thy sovereign grace.

1885.

LXXIX. . . . S. M.

"*For thy great mercies, O Lord, hear.*"—Dan. ix. 18, 19.

I.

O FATHER, for thy love!
    O Saviour, for thy grace!
O Comforter, as heaven above
    Be this thy dwelling-place.

II.

O for the promised gift!
    O for the gracious rain!
Let not thy church, O Lord, uplift
    Her hungering prayers in vain.

III.

O for the touch of power!
    O for the tongues of flame!
O for the coming of the hour
    To glorify thy name.

IV.

O for the tender heart!
O for the loving fear!
Blest Holy One, the gift impart
 Thy still, small voice to hear.

V.

Hasten the rising sun!
O drive away the night!
Soon may thy sovereign will be done,
 Thy kingdom come in might.

1885.

LXXX. . . . . 8, 7.

"Yet he bare the sin of many."—Isa. liii. 12.

I.

O THE darkness, O the sorrow,
    O the misery of sin!
When will dawn the promised morrow
    That shall bring deliverance in?

II.

One there was ordain'd to languish,
    Guiltless, in Gethsemane:
One there was who died in anguish,
    Innocent, on Calvary.

III.

Jesus was the burden-bearer,
    God's own Son the sacrifice,—
Of the griefs of man the sharer,
    Of his soul the ransom-price.

IV.

'Tis the Christ, the ever-living,
    Ever-loving, ever-blest,
By the Comforter still giving
    Pardon, holiness, and rest.

V.

Can the love so freely given,
    Can the blood so freely shed,
Fail to draw the earth to heaven,—
    Fail to bring alive its dead?

VI.

Rise, O children of the Father!
    Stand, ye brothers of the Son,
In unyielding ranks together
    Till the crown of Christ be won:

VII.

Till the lands of sin and sorrow,
    Darker than the ancient night,
Shall behold the promised morrow
    Beam on them with saving light.

1886.

LXXXI. .... 8, 9.

"Caught up into Paradise."—2 Cor. xii. 4.

I.

BEFORE the silver cord be loosed,
   Or e'er the golden bowl be broken,
   By Christ's redeem'd is heard and spoken
A language ne'er by earthlings used.

II.

While waiting for his call of grace,
   The links of life as yet unriven,
   A new-created sense is given
That pierces the immeasured space.

III.

The spirit, newly clothed upon,
   Out-reaches to the gates eternal,
   And glimpses of the realms supernal
Eclipse awhile the natural sun.

IV.

So Stephen saw the Son of man
    At God's right hand enthroned in glory,
    And while with martyr-baptism gory
His life on high with Christ began.

V.

And so, through time's on-speeding years,
    Some ripening saints, with favour gifted,
    Anear God's presence have been lifted
While dwelling in these lower spheres.

VI.

Of old, the shepherds saw on high
    His angels in their bright apparel,
    And heard redemption's wondrous carol,
Alone, beneath the midnight sky.

VII.

If distant glories of the throne
    Transfigure now our earthly mansions,
    What powers, what insights, what expansions,
When we shall know as we are known!

1886.

LXXXII. . . . 8, 8.

"Thou makest the outgoings of the morning and evening to sing."
Ps. lxv. 8.

I.

Day is waning into shadow;
　Darkness dims the hill and meadow,
Till the stars light up the even
As they climb the hills of heaven.

II.

With its lantern earthward swinging,
See the firefly heavenward winging;
While from crannied wall and thicket
Comes the carol of the cricket.

III.

Peace, with hushing finger lifted,
Cheers the heart by sorrow rifted,
Pointing to the Comfort-Giver
And the home beyond the river.

IV.

As an island ocean-bounded,
Lord, thy love hath me surrounded,—
Love in sunlight, love in showers,
Bringing precious fruits and flowers.

V.

Thou hast given from thy treasure
Bounties more than I can measure:
Yea, my Father! not a minute
But has come with goodness in it.

VI.

Years there were that brought me crosses;
Times of pain and grief and losses;
Still they carried in their keeping
Sowing-time and harvest-reaping.

VII.

As the span of life shall lengthen,
Lord, my faith and patience strengthen:
Daily to thee bring me nearer,
Daily to me be thou dearer.

VIII.

After thine, O holy Saviour!
Pattern'd be my life's behaviour:
Less of self in all my bearing,
More for others daily caring.

IX.

When shall come the soul's undressing,
May I fall asleep with blessing,
And await thy call of waking
When the heavenly day is breaking.

X.

Past all earthly joy and weeping,
What a waking after sleeping,
When the new-born eye beholdeth
What thy grace, dear Lord, unfoldeth!

1886.

LXXXIII. . . . . 8, 7.

To them that love God all things work together for good.
Rom. viii. 28.

I.

COLD the bed and hard the pillow,
  Yet the wanderer slept near heaven:
Wild the wind and high the billow,
  Yet the bark was homeward driven.

II.

Bitter were the tears of sorrow,
  Yet the drops were turn'd to balm:
Darkly loom'd the dreaded morrow,
  Yet it broke in heavenly calm.

III.

Fiery darts above him flying,
  Yet beneath faith's shield he lay:
Weary paths before him lying,
  Yet a brook was by the way.

IV.

Heavy seem'd the cross unlifted,
    Yet 'twas light when taken up:
Empty was the rock unrifted,
    Yet a blessing fill'd the cup.

V.

Fierce the furnace sevenfold heated,
    Yet the Son of God was there:
By the evil ill-entreated,
    Yet the Lord his sorrow bare.

VI.

Often worn and heavy-laden,
    Yet there came a perfect rest
When the soul, his promise stay'd on,
    In the Lord was ever blest.

1887.

LXXXIV. . . . . 8, 8, 8.

God, who giveth us richly all things to enjoy.—1 Tim. vi. 17.

I.

FATHER! all is of thy giving:
   All of good from thee receiving,
This the wherefore man is living:

II.

This the blessedness of being,
Led by thee, the One All-seeing,
In the ways of thy decreeing.

III.

By the power of thy Spirit,
Only in thy dear Son's merit,
Daily grace do we inherit.

IV.

On our upward journey going
In the strength of thy bestowing,
Building up or overthrowing:

V.

Overthrowing things of meanness,
In their prime or budding greenness,
Pride and passion and uncleanness:

VI.

Evil thought and evil speaking,
Words with hate and envy reeking,
Grasping greed and selfish seeking.

VII.

Building not of wood and stubble
Things that perish like a bubble
In the day of fiery trouble:

VIII.

But of gold and gems the rarest;
Stones the strongest and the fairest;
Earnest deeds for which thou carest:

IX.

Precious gems of love undying;
Patient, faithful, self-denying;
Sturdy stones that stand the trying.

X.

Not for honours transitory,
Not for name in passing story,
But to thy most sovereign glory.

XI.

Nor of our own wisdom, Master!
Else we work alone disaster:
Lord! be thou our life's forecaster.

XII.

This thy children's joy in living,
Kingly gifts from thee receiving,
Love and service to thee giving.

1888.

LXXXV..... S. M.

Let him sit alone, and keep silence, because He hath laid it upon him.
Lam. iii. 28.

I.

BE still, my soul! be still,
  Nor hide thee in the cleft;
But to thy Father's loving will
  Be thy deliverance left.

II.

But little dost thou know,
  But little canst thou see
Of the unfoldings of the plan
  That grasps eternity:

III.

That holds the child of days,
  That holds the angelic throng,
And spans the countless worlds that move
  Their starry path along.

IV.

Yet God will not forget
    The ransom'd of his grace:
The gift of his belovéd Son
    Doth every gift embrace.

V.

His mercy hovers round
    Thy pathway every hour:
His loving-kindness is as vast
    As his almighty power.

VI.

Be quieted, my soul!
    In sweet content abide:
If night be long, the day will come,
    And thou'lt be satisfied.

VII.

My soul! bless now the Lord,
    Thy hope, thy rock, thy King!
Thy Father, Saviour, Comforter,
    E'en in the darkness sing.

1889.

LXXXVI. .... 8, 7.

I will meditate also upon all thy work, and muse on thy doings.
Psalm lxxvii. 12.

I.

SITTING in the twilight musing
  On the days that come and go,
Joys and sorrows, interfusing,
  Mingled in a sunset glow:
All were of the Father's choosing,
  Gifts most fitting to bestow.

II.

Often had the sun been shining:
  Yet e'en when the day was chill,
Shower and sunshine, intertwining,
  Rainbows flung from vale to hill,
And the soul, its self resigning,
  In the peace of God lay still.

III.

When, the Saviour's voice unheeding,
  In the depths the spirit lies,

We see not the ladder leading
    Upward to the holy skies,
Till the Hand for us once bleeding
    Touch with sight our blinded eyes.

IV.

Evermore the Shepherd careth
    For the gather'd of his fold:
Still the wandering ones he beareth
    From the darkness and the cold:
Still he healeth, still he spareth,
    As on earth he did of old.

V.

O what loving pity bideth
    In the bosom of our Lord!
He that in His truth confideth
    Finds the treasure in it stored,
That for him His grace provideth
    An exceeding great reward.

VI.

Musing in the quiet chamber
    Of the soul at eventide,
If we stir some ashy ember
    Of a fire that long had died,
Penitent, may we remember
    Christ our Lord was crucified!

1889.

LXXXVII. . . . . L. M.

*For the Old Log College Celebration, near the Neshaming,
September 5, 1889.*

I.

STRENGTH of our fathers in the day
    A mighty work upon them lay,
Which thou hast crown'd with holy fame,
We bless and magnify thy name.

II.

A house for thee they builded well:
Though humblest in all Israël,
Yet thou didst sanctify as thine
The prophets' school of lore divine.

III.

The seed of truth in faith was sown:
Nurtured of thee, a tree hath grown
Whose branches overspread the land,
And thousands in its shadow stand.

IV.

Its fruits are knowledge, life, and light;
Knowledge of thee, so clear, so bright,
That he whose soul with truth is rife
Shall find in Christ eternal life.

V.

That tree, of verdure fresh and fair,
While mountains stand shall fruitage bear,
And in the garden of the Lord
Perennial blessings shall afford.

VI.

Jehovah-jireh! We adore
The God whose love provided more
Than they foreknew who sow'd in tears,
And reap'd in joy in after years.

VII.

Glory to God! our voices sing:
Glory to God! our praise we bring:
Glory to God! let all men cry:
Glory to God! let heaven reply.

1889.

LXXXVIII. .... 7's.

The Comforter, the Holy Spirit, whom the Father will send in my name, he shall teach you all things.—John xiv. 26.

I.

BUILDER of thy holy church:
  Comforter of all thy saints:
Guide of all that meekly search:
  Helper of the heart that faints:
    Holy Spirit! Lord divine!
    Gracious majesty is thine.

II.

Dweller in the lowly heart
  Clothed in faith's simplicity,
Unto us the grace impart
  Of thy loving flock to be.
    Holy Spirit! day by day
    Guide and keep us in thy way.

III.

Christ the Lord went up on high:
  Yet in thee he bideth here,

Right-hand of Infinity,
　　Till in judgment he appear:
　　　Holy Spirit! glorify
　　　Thine eternal majesty.

IV.

Not by works that man can do
　　Can the guilt of man be shriven:
Thou alone createst new,
　　Grace through thee alone is given:
　　　Holy Spirit! give us light
　　　To discern the truth aright.

V.

Sanctifier of thy church!
　　Cast out what is not of Thee:
Let no human touch besmirch
　　Thine own temple's purity.
　　　Holy Spirit! unto Thee—
　　　Not to man—all glory be.

VI.

Arm of everlasting strength,
　　Executing God's decrees!
Victor over all at length,
　　Thou wilt bring in perfect peace.
　　　Holy Spirit! God of power!
　　　Quickly come the glorious hour.

1890.

LXXXIX. . . . . 6, 8.

The bright, the Morning-Star.—Rev. xxii. 16.

I.

THE bright, the Morning-Star!
    Forerunner of the day,
The shadows flee afar
    Before its radiant way;
Dawn of an immortal morrow
On a world redeem'd from sorrow.

II.

Its uncreated rays
    Of never-fading sheen—
An endless day of days
    Without a night between—
Swifter fly than angel-pinions
Over measureless dominions.

III.

The Christ, the Morning-Star!
    How shadowy and how dim

The purest jewels are
    Mid light that beams from Him!
Brightness of the Father's glory!
Thine no radiance transitory.

IV.

O Christ, the Morning-Star,
    How beauteous art Thou!
Through heavenly gates ajar
    We catch some glimpses now:
O the joy, the love, the wonder,
When we pass the portals yonder!

V.

How long eternity!
    Yet not a foot will tire,
No hand hang wearily,
    And not a joy expire:
Eye undimm'd and soul unsated
E'er will find new joys created.

VI.

O Morning-Star! the light
    That lighteth every man,
Dispel the shades of night
    That fell when sin began.
Shine on all, O Star supernal!
Dayspring of the life eternal.

1891.

XC..... DIES IRÆ.

A Rendering in the Original Metre of the Latin Hymn of Thomas of Celano.

I.

DAY of wrath! the day that endeth
   Time, the world ablaze, impendeth!
So old prophecy portendeth.

II.

What the trembling consternation
When the Judge of all creation
Comes for strict investigation!

III.

Lo! the startling trumpet, swelling,
Through the graves its blast impelling,
Man before the throne is knelling!

IV.

Struck aghast both Death and Nature,
When upcometh every creature
To the dreaded judicature.

V.

Bringing forth the Book indited,
All the world's misdeeds recited
Rightfully will be requited.

VI.

When the Judge his seat assumeth,
What is secret he illumeth;
None escaping whom he doometh.

VII.

Woe is me! what exculpation?
Who can proffer mediation
Since the just scarce find salvation?

VIII.

King of majesty astounding!
With thy grace thine own surrounding,
Save me, Fount of love abounding!

IX.

Holy Lord! recall thy yearning
E'en when I thy ways was spurning:
Keep me on that day of burning!

X.

Waiting, weary, me thou soughtest:
On the cross my soul thou boughtest:
Not in vain be work thou wroughtest!

XI.

Judge avenging! with contrition
I entreat thy full remission
Ere that day of inquisition!

XII.

Wailing, as one self-accusing,
Guilt my crimson'd face suffusing,
Spare me, Lord! of thy good choosing.

XIII.

Mary was by thee forgiven,
And by thee the thief was shriven:
Let not hope from me be driven.

XIV.

Worthless all my prayers ascending,
Yet, thy grace benign extending,
Save me from the fires unending!

XV.

With thy sheep infold me ever
At thy right-hand, wandering never:
From the goats my portion sever.

XVI.

When the wicked, self-confounded,
Are by angry flames surrounded,
Be my name with blessing sounded.

XVII.

Prostrate, for thy mercy crying,
Heart as if in ashes lying,
Care for me when I am dying.

On that tearful day of terror,
 At the fiery resurrection
Judging man for sinful error,
 God, grant this one thy protection!

O kind Jesus, Lord and Saviour,
Give to them thy restful favour!
  Amen.

1891.

XCI. . . . . 8, 7.

In my Father's house are many mansions.—John xiv. 2.

I.

No tears for those whose feet have pass'd
    Within the golden portals,
Away their dusty garments cast
    For robes of the immortals.

II.

Out of the depths no more they cry,
    They sing upon the mountains;
No more in thirsty lands they sigh,
    They drink of living fountains.

III.

They look upon the face of One,
    Whom they had loved unseeing,
Who loved them in the ages gone,
    Before they were in being.

IV.

No idling part is theirs to fill
    In that high realm of splendor:
They go and come as God shall will
    And loving service render.

V.

At his behest, to sun or star
    They speed on viewless pinions,
To do his bidding near or far
    Throughout his wide dominions.

VI.

The trees of sinless knowledge grow
    In fields forever vernal:
The streams of love anear them flow
    Unfathom'd and eternal.

VII.

No days will measure holy time,
    No Sabbath once in seven;
The bells of gladness always chime
    In every heart in heaven.

VIII.

No lassitude will numb the brain,
    No heart nor hand grow weary;
No tear, no sigh, nor any pain,
    No night, no tempest dreary.

IX.

From mansions in that Paradise,
    With Jesus Christ forever,
Would we our parted ones entice
    To earth again?—No! never!

1891.

XCII. . . . . 7, 8, 8, 7.

The day is thine, the night also is thine.—Ps. lxxiv. 16.

I.

LORD of night as of the day!
While the lingering twilight paleth
And the evening-star prevaileth,
Quietly I muse and pray.

II.

Great thy goodness, Lord! how wide!
For thy loving-kindness twineth
Round each ray of light that shineth
From the morn till eventide.

III.

When the night is going by
Dewdrops gather without number,
So in my unconscious slumber
Countless blessings round me lie.

IV.

Spread thy sheltering wing to-night;
Let me sleep beneath its cover,
While unseen the angels hover
Near me till the morning light.

1891.

XCIII. . . . . L. M.

Come now, and let us reason together, saith the Lord: though your sins be as scarlet, they shall be as white as snow.—Isa. i. 18.

I.

I DID not ask the reason why
The Lord of life came here to die
   Until I found I needed one
   To do what Jesus Christ hath done.

II.

A lonely traveller in the dark,
The way unlighted by a spark,
   I stumbled onward with a dole
   Of sin and sorrow in my soul.

III.

The burden that within me lay
I saw not how to put away,
   Till one unseen spake tenderly,
   "Take up thy cross and follow me."

IV.

I took the cross he bade me take,
To bear it for his gracious sake:
    A willing power unknown before
    Each passing day possess'd me more.

V.

The hand that made me strong was such
I scarcely felt its gentle touch:
    To do his will, it was no cross;
    To follow him, it was no loss.

VI.

That loving one who spake to me,
The very God in Christ is he!
    O that the world would ask him why
    The Lord of life came here to die.

                            1892.

XCIV . . . . . C. M.

Behold, thy King cometh unto thee.—Matt. xxi. 5.

I.

A GLADSOME heart is mine this day;
    My thoughts within me sing;
A welcome guest has come to stay:
    'Tis Jesus Christ, my King!

II.

My house—an humble place it is—
    May be with little stored,
Yet it and all therein are his,
    For he is Christ, my Lord.

III.

He does not come, that Master mine,
    To tarry for a night,
For shelter at the day's decline,
    To go at morning light.

IV.

Nor does he as a king come in,
    Although my King is he:
He comes as one of brother-kin
    With brother's grace for me.

V.

He always gave me good for ill,
    And I ashamed could hide;
Yet more than brother is he still,
    My Father, Saviour, Guide.

VI.

How mean my barely-furnish'd rooms
    For such a gracious guest!
But at his touch a tent becomes
    A palace of the blest:

VII.

A palace on the border-line
    Betwixt the earth and skies,
Where in its windows light doth shine
    Across from Paradise.

VIII.

O Christ, my King! I cannot tell
    Why such a thing can be,
That thou wilt deign with me to dwell,
    As one beloved of thee!

1892.

XCV. ℒ . . . 8, 7.

The fool hath said in his heart, There is no God.—Ps. xiv. 1.

I.

DRIFTING on a lawless ocean,
    Toss'd by random-roving gales,
Not a helm to guide the motion,
    Not a hand to trim the sails:

II.

All uncertain whence or whither,
    Not a reckoning ever made,
Sweeping ever hither-thither,
    Not a course by compass laid:

III.

Not a log the speed to measure,
    Not a lookout on the mast;
Moving on at chance's pleasure,
    Yet to leeward trending fast:

IV.

Not a rock or shoaling charted,
  None to cast the warning lead,
Sunlight, starlight, both departed,
  Fog around and overhead:

V.

Not a cable nor an anchor,
  Ballast shifting as she sways.
Sheathing eaten off by canker,
  Rotting ratlins, shrouds and stays:

VI.

Hatches broken, timbers creaking,
  Pumps dismantled, lifeboat gone,
Water through the seams a-leaking,
  Creeping upward on and on:

VII.

Not a master to direct her,
  Not a watch to walk her deck,
Not a pilot to protect her,
  Not another craft at beck:

VIII.

What the fate of such a vessel
  Wandering over unknown deeps,
When with storm she comes to wrestle,
  When on her a cyclone sweeps?

IX.

What can help her as she driveth
    Through the breakers on the rock?
Who can rescue when she riveth
    Into fragments by the shock?

X.

Such the man who, God denying,
    Launches out into the night,
On himself alone relying;
    Not on Him who guideth right;

XI.

Man who puffs at God, his Master,
    As if God in Christ were not:
What for him but dread disaster?
    What but wreck his certain lot?

                      1892.

XCVI. .... 7's.

Christ shall reign for ever and ever.—Rev. xi. 15.

I.

WHO shall reign if not the Christ?
    Who can wield his wand of power?
Can the might of man suffice
    To uphold the spheres an hour?

II.

Who but Christ can seek and save?
    Who but he our pardon win?
Who but he can bridge the grave
    Heavenward from a world of sin?

III.

Who but Christ, the only Way,
    Only Truth, and only Life,
Out of darkness brings the day,
    Love and peace for woe and strife?

IV.

Christ his kingship will maintain:
    Every knee to him shall bow!
Glorious will be his reign:
    Lord! reveal thy glory now!

1892.

XCVII. .... 8, 5.

Behold, I stand at the door and knock.—Rev. iii. 20.

I.

WHO is he, my soul! that standeth
  At thine outer door?
What is it that he demandeth,
  Knocking evermore?

II.

In the night and in the morning,
  And through all the day;
It may be a friendly warning,
  Else why should he stay?

III.

Surely 'tis no jester, mocking
  With a false alarm:
There is something in the knocking
  That forewarneth harm.

IV.

'Tis perchance a friend appealing,
    For he gently knocks:
Not a robber, bent on stealing
    Spite of bar and locks.

V.

Hear his voice, "Lo! I am waiting,
    Waiting long have been:
Open wide the door and grating;
    Let thy Master in!

VI.

"From my locks the drops are falling,
    Drops of midnight dew:
I am waiting, I am calling,
    Lingering soul! for you!"

VII.

Jesus Christ, the King, in waiting!
    Christ, the Lord of all!
And I, fearful, hesitating
    To obey his call!

VIII.

Wondrous patience! love stupendous!
    Standing at thy door,
O my soul! thy loss tremendous
    If he knock no more.

IX.

Lo! the hinges, set and rusty,
    All my efforts mock:
And these bolts, disused and dusty,
    How can I unlock?

X.

Help me, Lord! I humbly pray thee
    For thy mercy's sake:
Every barrier that would stay thee
    Give me strength to break.

1892.

XCVIII. . . . . C. M.

The way of man is not in himself: it is not in man that walketh to direct his steps.—Jer. x. 23.

I.

How prone my hasty feet to stray
  Where fallen angels trod,
To shape for mine own self a way
  And be myself my God.

II.

How oft, Most High! I went about
  As though I plann'd my lot;
Thee, Sovereign Master! leaving out
  As if thou ruledst not.

III.

When cloudlessly the sun came up,
  'Twas at my beck it shone:
When blessings brimm'd my daily cup,
  My hand the boon had won.

IV.

When troubles came, my willing back
    I bent to take the load,
And stubbornly I bore the pack
    Along my chosen road.

V.

How oft I nurtured infant cares
    Till they became full grown;
How oft usurp'd thine own affairs
    To manage as mine own.

VI.

O Lord! my heart is slow to learn
    Faith's simple alphabet,
And dimly does my mind discern
    The lessons thou dost set.

VII.

O! take my wilful self from me,
    And give me, Lord! instead,
The mind that, trusting all to thee,
    Submissively is led.

1892.

XCIX. . . . . 7's.

Things which eyes saw not, and ears heard not.—1 Cor. ii. 9.

I.

Do the blest in Paradise,
    Crown'd with the immortal birth,
Sometimes bend their earnest eyes
    To the loved ones on the earth?

II.

From the starry battlements
    Do they spy the land away,
Where they dwelt in fragile tents,
    Habited in robes of clay?

III.

Do they, by permissive grace,
    To their olden home repair,
Take unseen their custom'd place
    In the seeming empty chair?

IV.

Hidden from us, do they walk
    Noiselessly beside us here,
And in silent whispers talk
    In the soul's receptive ear?

V.

As the fanning of a wing
    O'er a wan and fever'd brow,
Do they from its gardens bring
    Eden's zephyrs even now?

VI.

Are they sent to drive afar
    Things of darkness in the night,
While the bright, the Morning-Star
    Fills the soul with peace and light?

VII.

In the book of God are lines
    That no eye hath power to scan:
At his pleasure, his designs
    He unfoldeth unto man.

                          1892.

C. . . . . 6, 4.

For he is Lord of lords and King of kings.—Rev. xvii. 14.

I.

MY song of songs shall be
A hymn of praise to thee,
   O Christ my King!
Thy Father's gracious Son,
Thy church's precious one,
In whom its heaven is won,
   O Christ my King!

II.

How wondrous 'tis that God
In thee this earth hath trod,
   O Christ my King!
Divine effulgence thou,
His impress on thy brow,
To him in thee I bow,
   O Christ my King!

III.

Thou Lord of grace divine,
What lovingness is thine,
   O Christ my King!

Thou foilest Satan's arts,
Thou healest broken hearts,
All good thy hand imparts.
    O Christ my King!

IV.

In heaven I've none but thee:
In earth be all to me,
    O Christ my King!
Thy service my delight,
So glorious and so bright,
My joy shall have no night,
    O Christ my King!

V.

Thy kingdom shall remain;
Ne'er shall thy glory wane,
    O Christ my King!
Old earth shall pass away,
Its sovereigns turn to clay,
Eternal is thy sway,
    O Christ my King!

1892.

CI. . . . . 8, 5.

She said within herself, If I may but touch his garment, I shall be whole.—Matt. ix. 21.

I.

'TIS the Master standing yonder
    'Mid the pressing throng:
Some look on his face in wonder,
    Others pass along.

II.

He is teaching on the highways
    In the Holy Name,
Healing sufferers in the byways,
    Palsied, blind, and lame.

III.

E'en the dead becomes the living
    On the road to Nain:
Everywhere his hand is giving
    Help to souls in pain.

IV.

How my heart to him is reaching!
    More than man is he:
Gracious lessons he is teaching;
    O how sweet to me!

V.

O that I might kneel before him,
    With my feet unshod!
Trust him, love him, and adore him
    As my Lord and God.

VI.

Many years afflicted, needy,
    Spent is all my store:
If I find not succour speedy
    Hope is mine no more.

VII.

Long so friendless, homeless, lonely,
    Nothing can I pay:
I will touch his garment only,
    And will go my way.

VIII.

If I touch him, will he chide me?
    Will he help deny?
In the crowd I'll seek to hide me:
    I must touch or die!

IX.

Blessing from his garment floweth,
　　Even from its hem!
All its love my heart bestoweth:
　　Will he this contemn?

X.

He who giveth living water
　　When the heart is riven,
Healeth me, and saith: "My daughter!
　　Go in peace, forgiven."

1892.

CII. .... 8, 7.

He is the propitiation for our sins: and not for ours only, but also for the whole world.—1 John ii. 2.

I.

WHO the love of God can measure?
    Who dare set to him a bound?
Countless is the sum of treasure
    In the heavenly coffers found.

II.

Who would say, Thus far, no farther?
    Who would clip the wings of grace?
Shall we not to all men rather
    Tell how wide is God's embrace?

III.

Shall we, lingering in Judea,
    To Samaria be dumb?
Tell to none save in Berea
    Whosoever will may come?

IV.

Are there some beyond his pity?
    Has his heart no room for more?
Shall we round his holy city
    Build a wall without a door?

V.

Can we, in our fair apparel,
    Sit content in churches dim,
Hearing sermon, prayer, and carol,
    And the world so far from him?

VI.

Is the Holy Spirit waiting
    Till the church forsaketh sin,—
Dagons of its self-creating
    Casting down ere he come in?

VII.

With the harvest ripe for reaping,
    Shall the golden grain be lost?
Is it fitting time for sleeping
    At the eve of Pentecost?

VIII.

Lo! another century passes
    Shortly through the hundredth gate:
Must the world's ungather'd masses
    Wander till the hour too late?

1892.

PSALMS.

FOURTH PSALM.

L. M.

MY righteous God! O hear my call:
    For thou, of old, didst not forbear
Deliverance in my sore distress;
    O pity me, and hear my prayer.

Ye sons of man! how long will ye
    Pervert my glory into shame,—
Ye that love falsehood, seeking lies,
    To bring dishonour on my name?

But know, Jehovah for himself
    Hath set his chosen ones apart;
And when I call on him, he hears
    The cry that rises from my heart.

O rage no more, and cease from sin:
    Communing with your heart, be still:
Right sacrifices offer up,
    And trust ye in Jehovah's will.

The many say, "O that we might
    The time of good and plenty see!"
Lift thou, O Lord! on us the light
    Of thine own presence graciously.

Thou hast put gladness in my heart,
    More than they have from corn and wine:
In peace will I lie down and sleep,
    Thou, Lord, alone preservest thine.

1889.

FIFTH PSALM.

VERSES 1-3, 7, 8, 11, 12.

C. M.

GIVE ear unto my words, O Lord!
    And heed my yearning sigh:
My King, my God! O hear my voice,
    For unto thee I cry.

And in the morning, thou, O Lord,
    Shalt hear my voice arise:
At dawn will I set forth my prayer,
    And wait with watching eyes.

Through thy great loving-kindness, in
    Thy house will I appear,
And toward thy holy temple, Lord,
    Will worship in thy fear.

Lord, guide me in thy righteousness,
    So foes may rage in vain;
And make thy way before my face
    Lie open as a plain.

Let them be glad and shout for joy
    That refuge take in thee:
Defend thou them that love thy name,
    And let them joyful be.

Unto the righteous man, O Lord,
    Thy blessings e'er abound:
With favour dost thou compass him
    As with a shield around.

1889.

EIGHTH PSALM.

C. M.

O LORD, our Lord! in all the earth
    Thy name how excellent!
O let thy glory be inscribed
    Above the firmament!

Out of the mouth of very babes
    And sucklings dost thou build
A tower of strength by which the wrath
    Of vengeful foes is still'd.

When I behold thy heavens, O Lord,
    Thy finger-work divine,—
The moon and stars which thou hast set
    In their high place to shine,—

What is a mortal man, that him
    Thou in thy mind shouldst bear?
Or what a son of Adam's race,
    That thou for him shouldst care?

But little lower made than God,
    With fear and glory crown'd,
Dominion hast thou given to him
    Over thy works around;

Under his feet the creatures placed,
    The flocks and herds, yea all;
And on the wild beasts of the field
    His fear is made to fall:

The airy birds, the restless fish
    That through the waters sweep,
And whatsoever glideth through
    The pathways of the deep.

O Lord, our Lord! in all the earth
    Thy word of power didst frame,
How excellent the glory is
    Of thine eternal name!

                        1888.

TENTH PSALM.

L. M.

WHY standest thou far off, O Lord?
    Why hide thy face in troublous days?
The oppressor hotly hunts thy poor,
    And snares the men of lowly ways.

He praises yet despises God,
    What time his soul has won its greed:
There is no God in all his thoughts:
    The wicked saith, *He will not heed!*

His ways are strong and prosperous:
    Thy judgments high above his sight;
As for his adversaries all,
    He puffs at them in scornful spite.

He saith, *I never shall be moved;
    From age to age shall I be strong.*
Deceit and cursing fill his mouth,
    Mischief and wrong beneath his tongue.

He in the lurking-places hides:
  The innocent he slayeth there:
He waits in secret for his prey,
  A lion crouching in his lair.

He lurks until he catches them;
  The lowly in his net he draws;
Ensnared, they faint, and hopeless fall
  A prey within his cruel jaws.

He saith, *Their God remembereth not;*
  For He his face hath cover'd o'er!—
He saith it in his secret heart—
  He will not see forevermore.

Arise, Jehovah! Lift thou up
  Thy hand of wrath, Almighty God!
Forget not them that suffer wrong,
  The lowly ones on whom he trod.

Why doth the oppressor dare contemn
  The righteous God? Why hath he thought
Within his heart that thou wilt not
  Avenge the anguish he hath wrought?

YET THOU HAST SEEN! And in thy hand
  The grief, the trouble, thou dost take:
With thee the wretched leaveth it,
  The orphan'd thou wilt not forsake.

Lord! shatter thou the oppressor's arm;
    And as for the malignant one,
Search out, till, of his wickedness,
    Unrecompensed thou findest none.

Jehovah evermore is King!
    The heathen perish from his land!
Thou, Lord! hast heard the lowly cry,
    And thou wilt hold them in thy hand.

Thine ear will hear, thy hand defend,
    The helpless and the fatherless;
And man, of dust, shall nevermore
    Contemn thee, and thy poor oppress.

1891.

NINETEENTH PSALM.
7, 6.

THE heavens declare the glory
    Of their creator God;
The firmament revealeth
    His handiwork abroad.

Day unto day outpoureth
    Its speech in silent praise,
And night to night is breathing
    The knowledge of his ways.

Though speech be not, nor language,—
    Their voice none comprehend,—
Through earth their power extendeth,
    Their words go to its end.

A tent far in the heavens
    He setteth for the sun,
And there his rest he taketh
    What time the day is done.

He like a bridegroom steppeth
    Forth from his resting-place,
And boundeth like a warrior
    Again to run his race.

From heaven's extreme he speedeth
    Its circuit to complete;
And there is nothing hidden
    From his resistless heat.

Jehovah's law is perfect,
    The soul it rectifies;
And true his testimony,
    The simple making wise.

Right are Jehovah's precepts;
    They cause the heart to sing;
And clear is his commandment,
    The eyes enlightening.

His fear-compelling glory
    Forever shall endure;
And righteous are his statutes,
    Their truthfulness is sure:

Than gold more to be sought for,
    Fine gold that mines entomb,

And sweeter than the honey
    That droppeth from the comb.

Thy servant is instructed
    By them, most gracious Lord,
And in the keeping of them
    There is a great reward.

So high thy law, so holy,
    Who, of himself, can learn,
With all his inner searching,
    His errors to discern?

From faults unconscious clear me,
    And make me pure within;
Keep back thy servant also
    From all presumptuous sin.

Let it not have dominion,
    Then blameless I shall be,
And from the great transgression
    Thy grace shall hold me free.

My Rock and my Redeemer!
    Before thee be each word
And each heart-whisper'd musing
    Acceptable, O Lord.

1887.

FORTY-SIXTH PSALM.

7, 6.

A REFUGE and a fortress,
    Our God is on our side,
A very present helper
    When trouble doth betide.

Therefore, though earth be shaken,
    Our souls will never fear,
Though in the heart of oceans
    The mountains disappear.

What though the troubled waters
    In roaring foam shall break,
And their tumultuous swelling
    Shall make the mountains quake:
        The Lord of hosts is with us,
            Our refuge and our strength.

There is a heavenly river
    Whose streams shall never dry,
That gladdeneth God's city,
    The place of the Most High.

God in the midst of Zion
    Is evermore her stay;
Her he will help right early,
    E'en at the dawn of day.

The nations roar'd, the kingdoms
    Were riven to their base,
And when his voice he utter'd
    The earth did melt apace.
    The Lord of hosts is with us,
        Our refuge and our strength.

Behold Jehovah's doings,
    What wonders he hath wrought,
What awe-pervading silence
    On earth his hand hath brought.

The wars among the nations
    His word compels to cease,
And earth to all its borders
    He quieteth with peace.

The warrior's bow he shivers,
    The spear asunder rends;
The chariots he burneth
    Amid the fire he sends.

Be still; and know, ye nations,
    That I am God alone,
And I will be exalted
    O'er every land and throne.

The Lord of hosts is with us,
*   The God of Jacob is*
Our refuge and our fortress:
*   Be glory alway his!*

1888.

SIXTY-SECOND PSALM.

C. M.

ONLY in silence wait on God:
    My soul! thy help is He;
My rock, salvation, and defence,
    Unshaken I shall be.

How long will ye assail a man
    And hunt him as a prey,
Till he become a tottering wall,
    A fence that giveth way?

Their only thought to thrust him down,
    In lies is their delight:
While blessing with the mouth, their heart
    Doth curse with hidden spite.

Only in silence wait, my soul!
    My hope in God alone,
My rock, salvation, and high tower,
    I shall not be o'erthrown.

My glory and my help is God,
    My safeguard from all harm;
My refuge and my rock of strength
    Is his almighty arm.

O put your trust in him alway,
    Ye people who are his:
Pour out your heart before your God,
    For he our refuge is.

Only a breath are men; the sons
    Of nobly-born a lie;
For in the balance they go up,
    A breath of vanity.

Trust not in wrong, nor vainly boast
    The crafty spoiler's art;
And if your riches grow apace,
    On them set not your heart.

One thing hath God himself declared,—
    Yea, two things have I heard,—
That power belongeth unto God!
    Yet grace is in this word;

For loving-kindness, Lord, is thine,
    While justice rules thy thought;
Thou renderest to every man
    As he his work hath wrought.

1888.

EIGHTY-SIXTH PSALM.

C. M.

BOW down thine ear to me, O Lord!
   In mercy answer me:
Distress'd and needy, keep my soul,
   As one beloved by thee.

O thou, my God! thy servant save
   That trusteth thee in all:
Be gracious unto me, O Lord!
   So all day long I call.

Thy servant's soul make glad, O Lord!
   That thee I may extol;
For, O Jehovah! unto thee
   Do I lift up my soul.

How good and ready to forgive!
   How plenteous in grace
And loving-kindness unto all
   That seek, O Lord, thy face.

Give ear, Jehovah! to my prayer
    That goeth forth to thee,
And to my supplicating voice
    Attend thou graciously.

My heart cries out to thee alone
    When days of sorrow lower,
For thou wilt surely answer me
    In tribulation's hour.

Yea, there is none like unto thee
    Among the gods, not one!
Like thine there are no works, O Lord!
    The works thy hand hath done.

All nations, Lord! which thou hast made
    Shall come and worship thee,
And they shall glorify thy name,
    So great exceedingly.

For thou art great, and wondrous works
    Wrought by thy mighty hand
Show thou alone art God, whose throne
    Eternally shall stand.

Teach me thy way, and may thy truth
    My daily goings frame,
And knit my heart to thee, O Lord,
    So I may fear thy name.

With my whole heart, O Lord my God,
    I give thee thanks and praise,
And I will glorify thy name
    Through everlasting days.

Thy loving-kindness is so great
    I cannot set its bound:
My soul thou hast deliver'd from
    The depths beneath the ground.

Against me, Lord! the proud have risen,
    And men of violence,
Who set not thee before their eyes,
    Have sought to drive me hence.

But thou, Lord! art the mighty God,
    Compassionate and kind,
Long-suffering and full of truth,
    And gracious is thy mind.

Turn thee to me, thy favour show,
    And make thy servant strong:
The son of thy handmaiden save
    From men of guile and wrong.

Show me a token, Lord, for good,
    That those who hate may see
And be ashamed, because thy hand
    Hath cheer'd and holpen me.

1891.

NINETY-SECOND PSALM.

5, 6.

IT is a good thing
    To give thanks to the Lord,
To sing to thy praise
    In a tuneful accord:

Thy love to show forth
    In the morning, Most High!
Thy faithfulness also
    As night goeth by:

On the ten-stringëd lute
    And the tremulent lyre,
While rapturous musings
    The harp doth inspire.

By thy doings, Jehovah!
    Thou gladdenest me:
By the work of thy hands
    I am joyful in Thee.

Thy doings how great!
    And thy thoughts how profound!
The brutish know not,
    Nor can a fool sound.

When the wicked spring up
    As the grass after rain,
And the workers of evil
    Do prosper amain,

'Tis that, in due time,
    They shall wither and die:
But thou, O Jehovah!
    Art ever Most High.

Thine enemies perish
    As things of unworth,
And they that work evil
    Are scatter'd on earth.

My horn thou hast raised
    As the wild ox's horn:
Fresh oil of anointing
    My head doth adorn.

Mine eyes shall behold,
    And mine ear also hear,
The wicked waylayers
    Dispersing in fear.

The righteous shall blossom
    Like a palm in its pride,
And grow like the cedars
    On Lebanon's side:

For they that be planted
    Where thou art adored
Shall spring up and bloom
    In the courts of the Lord.

In hoary old age
    They shall still ripen fruit;
Fat and green they shall be,
    Full of sap from the root.

For Jehovah is upright:
    My stronghold is He:
Yea, righteous forever
    Jehovah will be!

                              1890.

NINETY-THIRD PSALM.

8, 7.

EVERMORE Jehovah reigneth!
    He is clothed with majesty:
He the worlds of worlds sustaineth
By the laws his will ordaineth:
    Girt about with strength is He!

Naught can shake his throne of glory,
    Stablish'd on infinity:
Let the floods lift up their roaring,
Billows over billows pouring,
    Glorious in his might is He!

Mightier is the Lord Jehovah
    Than the breakers of the sea:
Let them shout with voice of thunder,
Let them dash on rocks asunder,
    Lord omnipotent is He!

Steadfast are thy testimonies,
    Sure through all eternity:
In them truth its fullness summeth:
Holiness thy house becometh,
    Lord, forever! Praise to Thee!

1890.

NINETY-SEVENTH PSALM.

L. M.

JEHOVAH reigns! Let earth rejoice;
    And let the multitude of isles
Be glad, and sing with tuneful voice,
    And nature's face be clad in smiles.

Though clouds and darkness from afar
    Are round about his presence known,
Yet righteousness and judgment are
    The habitation of his throne.

A fire before him goes, and burns
    His enemies on every side;
His lightnings flash; and earth by turns
    Beholds and trembles in its pride.

The hills before his presence melt,
    Like wax before the furious flame;
His presence by the earth is felt
    Who built her everlasting frame.

The heavens declare his righteousness,
    The people all his glory see;
While they who serve the images,
    And boast in them, confounded be.

Then Zion heard, and she was glad;
    The daughters of Judea sang
Rejoicingly, and through the land
    The praises of thy judgments rang.

For thou, O Lord! above the earth
    Art high; thou art exalted far
Above the kings of mortal birth,
    Though lofty their aspirings are.

Hate evil, ye that love the Lord,
    For he preserves the saintly soul;
And every danger he will ward,
    And save from wicked men's control.

On righteous men shall light arise,
    Like morning breaking o'er the hills;
And hope shall kindle in their eyes,
    While holy mirth their bosom fills

Rejoice, ye righteous, in the Lord!
    Give thanks before his presence now;
In memory of his faithful word
    And holiness, give thanks, and bow.

1853.

ONE HUNDREDTH PSALM.

C. M.

HO, all ye lands! right joyfully
    Shout to the Lord your King:
Serve him with gladness, and before
    His gracious presence sing.

Know ye the Lord is God indeed:
    He made us: his we are,
His people; we the folded flock
    Within the shepherd's care.

O go your way into his gates,
    And glad thanksgivings raise;
Enter into his courts with songs,
    The songs of joyful praise.

Give thanks to him and bless his name,
    For always good is He!
His loving-kindness and his truth
    Endure eternally.

1890.

ONE HUNDRED AND TWENTY-FIRST PSALM.

6's.

I LIFT my longing eyes
   Up to the hills in vain:
Whence shall my help arise
   In time of want and pain?

My help is from the Lord
   Who gave all creatures birth,
And by his forming word
   Created heaven and earth.

No lurking enemy
   Thy foot shall turn astray,
For he that keepeth thee
   Will slumber not for aye.

Behold, he who in love
   Doth Israel ever keep,
His watchfulness shall prove,
   And slumber not nor sleep.

Thy keeper is the Lord,
    Jehovah is thy shade
On thy right hand: his word
    Thy sure defence is made.

By day the fervid sun
    Thy head shall never smite,
Nor shall the sickly moon
    Assail thee in the night.

Preserving thee from harm,
    All evil he'll control;
And his most gracious arm
    Shall e'er preserve thy soul.

When thou dost outward go,
    His grace shall go before;
In coming in also,
    Now and forevermore.

1871.

ONE HUNDRED AND FORTY-FIFTH PSALM.

C. M.

I WILL extol thee every day,
   My God, O glorious King;
And I will bless thy name for aye,
   Thy praise forever sing.

Great is the Lord and wonderful,
   And greatly to be praised:
His greatness is unsearchable,
   Beyond the heavens raised.

One generation, praising thee,
   Shall testimony bear
Unto the next, and wonderingly
   Thy mighty acts declare.

The honour of thy majesty,
   Thy wonders I'll proclaim;
Thine acts of terror men shall see
   And glorify thy name.

The memory of thy goodness they
    Shall utter far and wide;
Thy righteousness from day to day
    Shall sing on every side.

The Lord is gracious; full of kind
    Compassion: he is slow
To anger, and his holy mind
    Is great in mercy too.

The Lord our God is good to all,
    For all are in his thought;
His tender mercies richly fall
    On all that he hath wrought.

Thy works shall praise thee evermore,
    And thee thy saints shall bless;
Thy kingdom's glory and thy power
    To all the world confess;

Thy mighty acts that all may know
    Among the sons of men,
Thy kingdom's majesty to show
    To every creature's ken.

An everlasting kingdom's thine,
    And thy dominion sure

Throughout all generations' time
    Shall everywhere endure.

The Lord upholdeth all that fall,
    The bow'd with sorrow riven;
While on thee wait the eyes of all,
    Their meat is duly given.

Thou openest thy hand of grace,
    And thou dost satisfy
The wants of all in every place
    Who for thy presence cry.

The Lord is righteous in his ways,
    His works are holy all:
He's nigh to those that love his praise,
    And on him truly call.

The strong desire he will fulfil
    Of them that fear his name:
He hears their cry, and he will still
    Save them from harm and shame.

The Lord preserveth them from harm
    Who love him as their joy,
But wicked men his wrathful arm
    Will utterly destroy.

My mouth shall joyfully proclaim
    His praise from day to day:
Let all flesh bless his holy name
    Forever and for aye.

1871.

DOXOLOGIES.

L. M.

ALL praise to Thee, the Holy One,
    The Holy Father, Holy Son,
And Holy Spirit! Thou alone
Art King on the eternal throne.

C. M.

O HOLY, holy, holy Lord,
    The Father and the Son
And Holy Ghost! Be thou adored
    While endless ages run.

S. M.

BESIDE Thee there is none:
    Eternal God and King,
The Father, Son, and Holy Ghost,
    Thy glorious praise we sing.

7, 6.

THY love, O Holy Father,
    Thy grace, O Holy Son,
Thy peace, O Holy Spirit,
    Thy church abide upon:
While she her voice upraises
    To thine eternal throne,
And chants in endless praises
    Glory to God alone.

8, 7.

GLORY be to God the Father:
    Halleluiah!
  Glory be to God the Son,
    Halleluiah!
And to God the Holy Spirit,
    Halleluiah!
  In eternal being one!
    Halleluiah!
May his kingdom come in power;
    Halleluiah!
  And his holy will be done:
    Halleluiah!
  Halleluiah in the highest!
  Halleluiah evermore!

7's.

Glory to Thee evermore!
　Glory in the uttermost!
Heaven and earth thy name adore,
　Father, Son, and Holy Ghost.

8, 7, 4.

Glory in the highest! glory!
　Father, Son, and Holy Ghost:
King eternal! we adore thee,
　　Singing with the heavenly host,
　　　Glory! glory!
　Glory be to God on high!

Finis.

www.ingramcontent.com/pod-product-compliance
Lightning Source LLC
Chambersburg PA
CBHW021344230426
43666CB00006B/401